RAIL CENTRES:
NEWCASTLE

RAILCENTRES:
NEWCASTLE

K. HOOLE

Nottingham
Booklaw Publications

If the North Eastern Railway, its predecessors or its successors, interest you then why not join the North Eastern Railway Association? The Association was formed in 1961 to cater for enthusiasts and railwaymen interested in the railways of north eastern England. Details of membership can be obtained from the Membership Secretary, 48 Earlsdon Avenue, Middlesbrough, Cleveland TS5 8JR. Please enclose a SAE.

First published 1986 by Ian Allan Ltd

©Ian Allan Ltd 1986

This edition published 2008 by Booklaw Publications 382, Carlton Hill, Nottingham NG4 1JA

ISBN 1-901945-18-9

Printed by
The Amadeus Press, Cleckheaton, West Yorkshire

Contents

1 Early History

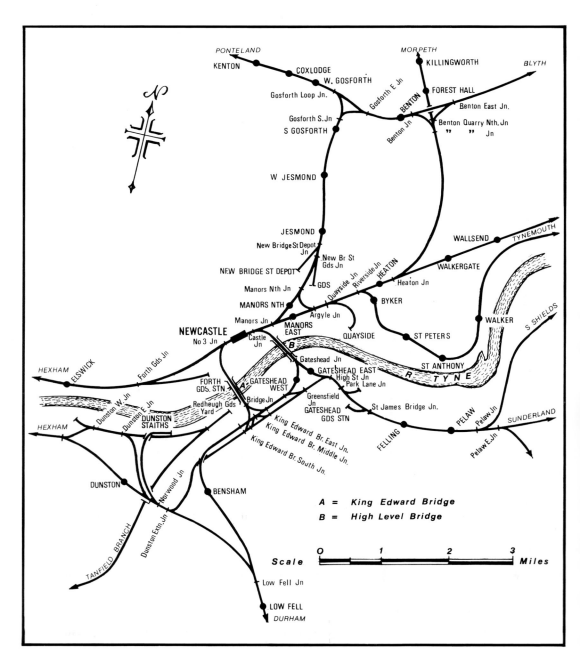

A = King Edward Bridge
B = High Level Bridge

Scale

0   1   2   3   Miles

The railway history of Newcastle is in some ways very complex. The city cannot be dealt with in isolation and our survey must take in Gateshead, on the opposite bank of the Tyne, and the numerous conurbations along both banks of the river — mainly to the east of the Newcastle/Gateshead hub, though including some to the west. Although the first public railways on both sides of the river were opened in the 1830s — the Newcastle & Carlisle, the Newcastle & North Shields, and the Brandling Junction (Gateshead to South Shields and Sunderland) — there had been railways in the area for many years previously. To start with there were the early wooden wagonways, later with a metal strip on the surface of the wooden rails to cut down the wear and tear on the timbers, and as technology developed there came the iron rail. In this work it is impossible to cover the long and complicated history of the waggonways, which spanned a period of some three centuries, and thus only public railways are dealt with. However, there is some mention of the more important industrial lines that connected with the NER and LNER.

Attempts to provide cheaper and more efficient haulage by steam power went on apace in the early years of the 19th century, notably in the Wylam area, and this led to the development of Newcastle and Gateshead as locomotive building centres. The most famous concerns were those of Robert Stephenson & Co, where *Locomotion* was built in 1825 for the Stockton & Darlington Railway, and R. & W. Hawthorn, established in 1817 to build marine engines. Across the river in Gateshead J. Coulthard & Son built a few locomotives, but in 1865 the Coulthard premises were taken over by Black, Hawthorn & Co and more than 1,000 locomotives were built by the new concern, mainly for British industrial railways, and railways overseas. On the closure of Black, Hawthorn & Co in 1896 ownership passed to Chapman & Furneaux, but closure came after a few years and the goodwill, patterns, etc were purchased by R. & W. Hawthorn Leslie & Co Ltd, successors to the Newcastle firm mentioned above. There were other firms which built a handful of locomotives in the early days of steam but which did not survive for long.

The two public railways serving the area to the east of Newcastle — the Newcastle & North Shields on the north bank, and the Brandling Junction on the south — were of only local importance, whereas the Newcastle & Carlisle Railway provided an important cross-country link. It was not until George Hudson came on

Far left:
Route Map of the Newcastle area as in 1915.

Below:
The portico — actually a porte-cochère — at Newcastle Central station in 1950. The tender of Scott & Reid was accepted on 21 November 1862 at a figure of £5,428 and the structure was completed in the following year. This was a much simpler version than that envisaged by Dobson when he designed the station in the 1840s. *BR*

Right:
The interior of the station about 1860. The platform in the foreground eventually became No 4. Note the curve of the roof, and the three-compartment coaches in two colours; first and second class coaches were painted with white upper panels and dark plum lower panels. The stage coach styling is apparent. *BR*

Facing page, top:
When opened in 1850 the station had a three-span roof; this 1880s view was taken at the east end, with the centre and north spans of the roof visible on the left.
K. Hoole Collection

Facing page, bottom:
The circulating area looking east to platforms 4 and 5. The station offices and services line the north wall (left) with wooden structures dotted about the concourse.
K. Hoole Collection

the scene and linked Gateshead with Darlington, York and London in 1844 that the possibility of Newcastle becoming an important centre on the London to Edinburgh line became a distinct probability. Fortunately George Stephenson's son, Robert, was at the height of his career and in 1849 his magnificent High Level Bridge across the Tyne gorge was opened for road and rail traffic, for which it is still used to this day.

Until 1906 the High Level Bridge was the only main line rail crossing and this meant that London-Edinburgh trains had to reverse in Newcastle Central station — a feature which had previously bedevilled York, where a new station opened in 1877 made through-running possible. The King Edward Bridge, opened in 1906, allowed trains from the south to enter Newcastle Central at the west end and leave for the north from the east end, greatly easing the working of the station, not to mention light engine and empty stock move-

ments. Newcastle Central station is actually sited on an east and west axis, parallel to the river.

The introduction of electric trams to the streets of Newcastle in 1901 resulted in a sharp decrease in passengers using the local stations which cost the NER dearly. This brought about the decision to electrify the lines along the north bank of the Tyne which served the coastal resorts of Tynemouth, Cullercoats, Whitley Bay and Monkseaton; although electrification of the south bank lines was proposed in 1908, 30 years were to pass before the scheme was implemented. Now British Rail's concern in the operation of these electrified lines has ceased completely and the passenger services are all provided by the Tyne & Wear Metro, mainly over what were originally NER routes, but including an underground cross-city section linking the Metro lines on the north bank with those on the south — an important link missing in NER

and LNER days. Consequently BR's remaining passenger services are limited to the London-Newcastle-Edinburgh and Newcastle-Carlisle routes, with some trains using the main line to York and then running to southwest England, or to Manchester and Liverpool, as successors to services established in the days of competition before 1914.

Although the inaugural train from London (Euston Square) to Gateshead on 18 June 1844 took only 9hr 21min for the journey (including stops totalling 70min) it was run under special conditions and the normal journey time was 12hr 30min (with stops totalling 165min). From 1 November 1844 the overall time was reduced to 12hr 15min on one train, the 9.00am from London, but *Bradshaw's Monthly Railway and Steam Navigation Guide* for July 1847 shows that by that date the sole express of the day, the 9.25am from Euston Square, was due in Newcastle (actually Gateshead) at 6.05pm — representing a total journey time of 8hr 40min.

The York to Gateshead section was covered in 135min with stops at Darlington and Durham. Over the years the journey time has been gradually reduced and in 1935 the 'Silver Jubilee' streamlined train was booked to cover the 268¼ miles in exactly 4hr, with a stop at Darlington. Now the 10.30am from King's Cross covers the distance in 173min at an average speed of 93mph!

The motive power has progressed from the primitive engines of the 1840s, through the Fletcher, Worsdell and Raven periods of the NER, to the famous Gresley engines, notably the Pacifics, of the LNER, which were themselves replaced by the powerful and noisy 'Deltic' diesels. Now we have the IC125 trains, with electrification to come in the fairly near future.

Mineral traffic from the once numerous collieries along both banks of the Tyne brought prosperity to the NER but is now virtually extinct, although a few large col-

lieries are still working on the coast north and south of the Tyne. The once familiar sight of North Eastern 0-6-0s and 0-8-0s plodding along with trainloads of coal in unbraked wagons has gone for ever.

The piecemeal development of the line between Darlington and Newcastle, which had to be used by both slow-moving mineral trains and the London-Edinburgh expresses, was not entirely satisfactory, and as early as July 1846 plans were announced for a line from Newcastle to the south running further to the west via the Team Valley. An Act for such a line was obtained in 1848 but was not followed up, and a second Act was necessary in 1862 when it was decided that a Team Valley line would have to be built because of the heavy traffic on the old main line. However, this line was not envisaged as passing through Durham but rather as joining the Gateshead-Ferryhill line near Belmont, east of Durham. A further look at the problem revealed that by building a second length of line from Relly Mill (south of Durham) to Hoggersgate Junction (north of Ferryhill and subsequently renamed Tursdale Junction) a completely new route from Gateshead to Ferryhill could be provided which would be free of the restrictions on the original line. Consequently the Gateshead to Durham section was opened in 1868, with only four local trains daily between Newcastle and Durham. With the completion of the southern section in 1872, however, the new route was available for through traffic and in fact developed into the East Coast main line we know today.

To the north of Newcastle the line to Berwick was completed when Queen Victoria opened the Royal Border Bridge across the Tweed on

29 August 1850, although a temporary bridge had been in use since 10 October 1848. At last it was possible to travel by train between London, York, Newcastle and Edinburgh. Here again both the route and the bridge are still in use for the faster and heavier trains of today.

Preceding the main line from north to south was the east to west Newcastle & Carlisle Railway which was opened in sections from 1834, originally terminating at its east end on the Gateshead side of the Tyne, but later reaching the Forth area of Newcastle (in 1847), with an extension to the new Central station in 1851. Next came the Newcastle & North Shields Railway, opened from a small station at Manors on 22 June 1839, closely followed by

the Brandling Junction Railway between Gateshead and Sunderland on 5 September 1839. The former was extended to Tynemouth in 1847 and eventually formed part of the North Tyne circle utilising a new (1882) line north of Tynemouth, and the 1864 Blyth & Tyne line into Newcastle with an independent terminus at New Bridge Street. The Brandling Junction Railway later reached South Shields and provided a route from Brockley Whins into Gateshead for trains arriving from the south via the Durham Junction and Stanhope & Tyne lines, which crossed the Brandling Junction line on the level at Pontop Crossing.

The success of the early railways led to a flood of proposals to build lines from anywhere to everywhere, and many were from companies which included the word 'Newcastle' in their title but which did not actually reach Newcastle; they merely provided connecting lines between other companies, one of which did reach Newcastle! Such railways were the Newcastle & Leeds Direct; the Newcastle & Hawick; the Newcastle, Shotley Bridge & Weardale Junction ; the Direct Newcastle & Durham & Great North of England Extension; the Lancaster & Newcastle Direct; and the Scarborough, Whitby, Stockton-on-Tees & Newcastle and Northern Junction Railway.

Other companies included Northumberland in their title and there were two Northumberland Railway companies; the first, in 1835, proposed a line to run from Newcastle to Morpeth, and the second, in 1843, one to run from Gateshead to Tweedmouth which was to be operated on the atmospheric principle.

When George Hudson brought the main line from the south to Gateshead he built a

Top:
The most famous engines on the East Coast main line were the Gresley Pacifics and this is Haymarket's No 4497 *Golden Plover* **being coupled to its train at platform 8 at Newcastle.**
W. B. Greenfield

Above:
When Pacifics were not available two North Eastern Atlantics were used — a practice that continued well into the 1930s. In this view the leading engine is 'C7' No 735 and the train engine is a 'C9', either No 727 or 2171, which by this time had lost its booster. *W. B. Greenfield*

magnificent station looking across the river to Newcastle, but the building of the High Level Bridge made this station redundant, so that within a few years it was converted to a locomotive repair shop and it remained in such use for more than a century. Now it has gone without trace. On the other hand the station which replaced it, Newcastle Central, is still in use and is, in fact the hub of the Tyneside long-distance rail traffic. Extensions carried out over the years brought its number of platforms to 15, but some are now out of use due to the withdrawal of the electric and other local services. Nevertheless the station is a fine tribute to rail transport on Tyneside — and long may it continue to be so.

For more than 130 years Central station has been one of the most notable buildings in the city; it is a fine example of early railway architecture, with the buildings on the north side, and much of the roof, dating back to the opening in 1850. Since then it has been extended at various times, both at the east end and on the south side.

The station was built to the designs of John Dobson, and the contract for the buildings was let to Messrs Mackay & Read on 14 August 1847 at a price of £92,097; but all was not well and as a result of the findings of a Committee of Investigation it was decided to suspend the construction of the elaborate portico, arcades and the hotel envisaged by Dobson. Tenders for the roof of the station were called for in

April 1849 and the station was opened by Queen Victoria and Prince Albert on 29 August 1850; the York, Newcastle & Berwick Railway's public services commenced the following day.

Contemporary accounts of the opening were full of praise for the design and the workmanship, although at least one newspaper described the station as planned (with portico, etc) and not as actually built. The Royal party arrived from Castle Howard at 12.47pm and, after an address by the Mayor of Newcastle, were invited to take lunch before proceeding to Berwick to open the Royal Border Bridge.

The west end of the station was operated separately under its own stationmaster and with its own staff; there was also a separate entrance from Neville Street, with its own booking office. This part of the station opened on 1 January 1851, with the extension of the Newcastle & Carlisle line from its previous terminus at Forth.

The present portico at Central station was erected in 1862/63 by Messrs Scott & Reid, the contract price being £5,428.

Below:
The 'Deltics' were worthy successors to the 'A4s' and on 13 July 1981 No 55009 *Alycidon* **was photographed ready to take over from No 55022** *Royal Scots Grey* **on the 07.36 Plymouth to Edinburgh train standing at platform 8.**
Ian S. Carr

In 1836 Richard Grainger published a pamphlet entitled 'A Proposal for Concentrating the Termini of the Newcastle & Carlisle, the Great North of England, and the Proposed Edinburgh Railways; and for Providing Spacious and Eligible Depots, With Convenient Access, from these Railways to the Town of Newcastle'. He envisaged the Newcastle & Carlisle Railway, The Great North of England Railway, and the proposed Brandling Junction line meeting south of the river and crossing the Tyne on a low level bridge to meet up with 'The Intended Railway to Edinburgh' at a proposed general depot at Elswick. Nothing came of his scheme at the time, but it may have sown a seed because some years later Newcastle acquired a fine new Central station.

The 1845 Act for the Newcastle & Berwick Railway included powers for a line from Gateshead (where it joined the Brandling Junction), across the Tyne to Neville Street,

Key to plan: **(A)** Entrance: **(B)** Station Master's Office; **(C)** Lost luggage store; **(D)** Waterclosets and urinals; **(E)** Second class Gentlemen's waiting room; **(F)** Second class Ladies' waiting room; **(G)** First class Gentlemen's waiting room; **(H)** First class Ladies' waiting room; **(I)** First class Ladies' refreshment room; **(J)** First class general refreshment room; **(K)** Bar; **(L)** Second class refreshment room; **(M)** Kitchen and scullery; **(N)** Pantry and store room; **(O)** Bar sitting room; **(P)** Store room; **(Q)** Waiters' sitting room; **(R)** Waiters' bedroom; **(S)** Ladies' attendants' room; **(T)** Washing room for first class Ladies; **(U)** Water closets and washing rooms for second class Ladies; **(1)** Booking office; **(2)** Parcels' office; **(3)** Lamp room; **(4)** Oil room; **(5)** Porters' room; **(6)** Engineer's office; **(7)** Engineer's pay office; **(8)** Clerks' office; **(9)** Urinals and water closets; **(10)** Stationmaster's house; **(11)** Store houses; **(12)** Telegraph office.

Note: The separate hotel block at the east end of the station buildings in the plan was not built until 1892. Until then limited hotel accommodation was provided in conjunction with the refreshment rooms, as at other early stations in the North-East.

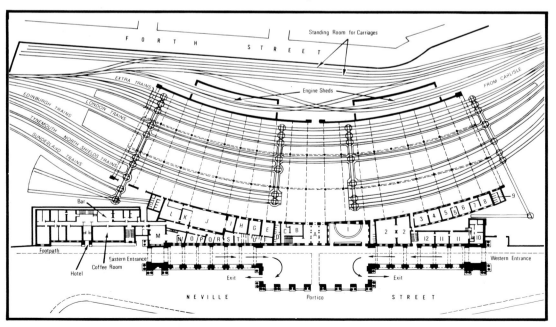

where it was planned to build the new Central station.

In December 1848 the *Civil Engineer & Architect's Journal* published a detailed description and plan of the building then under construction which, it was expected, would handle 140 arrivals and departures daily. The point was made that the site chosen was convenient for the centre of the town, and one where there was space for extensions if they became necessary. Another interesting point made by the contributor was that 'The identity of the central points of the great railway system of this period with the central points of the military occupation of the country by the Normans has been, in many instances, strikingly exemplified; and in none more so than at York, Newcastle and Berwick, in each of which towns the railway station closely adjoins the Castle'. It would be remarkable if there was any reader of this book who has not seen a photograph of the east end of Newcastle Central station with the Keep of the Castle in the background, or indeed a view of the east end of the station taken from the top of the Keep itself.

The text describes the 200ft-long portico (which was not built), with seven arches 14ft wide and 32ft high, divided by Doric columns 29ft high and standing on a base 7ft 6in high. On each side was an arcade for carriages and pedestrians, each 200ft long and with six 14ft-wide arches. Although the rear wall of the arcade was straight, the adjoining station buildings were curved on their south side, forming the segment of a circle of 800ft radius.

The train shed was 708ft long by 183ft wide, covering an area of 14,426sq yd, or approximately three acres, with an iron and glazed roof in three spans of 61ft 4in, supported on columns 23ft high and 33ft apart — although quoted as 50ft on the plan. The platforms at the east end are described as for Sunderland trains, Tynemouth and North Shields trains, Edinburgh trains and London trains, five of them being dead-end platforms with a turnplate at the buffer stops; there was also one through road to the Newcastle & Carlisle station at the west end, and three through roads for extra trains. Adjoining the south wall were two engine sheds.

At the west end there were three bay platforms all ending in turnplates. The plan also shows the proposed hotel at the east end, 190ft long by 66ft deep, which would have had 70 bedrooms, but this was not built. However, when the refreshment rooms were completed in 1852, 30 bedrooms and eight sitting rooms were provided on the upper floors.

The station was extended on the south side in 1871 by the addition of an island platform but originally through running to the Newcastle & Carlisle end of the station was not possible. In 1893 the roof on the south side was extended and the 1871 island platform was resited and became the present platforms Nos 9 and 10, with a large block of buildings down the middle. At the same time the line from Manors to Central was doubled and this required the duplication of the viaduct on which the line is carried. This joined up with the already widened section between Manors and Heaton, which had been converted from two to four tracks in 1887.

At the east end platforms 1, 2 and 3 were

Above:
Newcastle Central had virtually no carriage standing facilities and sets had to be worked empty to or from Heaton Carriage Sidings or Scotswood Bridge Sidings. Many types of engines were used, some spending all day on such duties, with some engines from out-of-town sheds filling in before returning home. This is 'J21' No 1819, a Gateshead engine, at the west end of Central station. *K. Hoole Collection*

Above left:
Class H1 4-4-4T No 2144, also at the west end, was photographed taking water at platform 9 in the 1930s; it was rebuilt to Class A8 in March 1935.
K. Hoole Collection

Left:
'A2' No 516 *Hycilla* working its own empty train from Heaton Carriage Sidings and entering platform 9, with some of the No 1 box staff watching the photographer!
K. Hoole Collection

Top:
When the first BR diesel electric No D201 worked the 10.00am from Kings Cross on 21 June 1958 it worked back from Newcastle on the 5.00pm — a turn-round time of only 135 minutes which would have been unthinkable with a steam locomotive. However, non-availability of diesel locomotives meant that the steam locomotive turned out as a replacement had to do the same and for six consecutives weeks 'A4' No 60022 *Mallard* performed this duty. She is seen here on 13 April 1960, with the reversed 'Flying Scotsman' headboard on the centre lamp bracket. *Ian S. Carr*

Above:
An unusual empty stock working occurred when two empty trains from Heaton Carriage Sidings were running in the wrong order on 27 June 1977. The stock for the 16.15 to Liverpool was behind that for the 16.28 to Cardiff, and Class 45 No 45043 *The King's Own Royal Border Regiment* on the latter train was diverted behind Central station, over the King Edward Bridge, back across the Tyne on the High Level Bridge and into the station, by which time the Liverpool train had been platformed, loaded, and sent on its way. *Ian S. Carr*

Above:

Newcastle's famous east end diamond crossings with a Pullman train entering platform 8, electric trains in platforms 1, 2 and a 'J72' pilot awaiting its next shunt. A 'V1' or 'V3' 2-6-2T is running light alongside the Pullman, travelling in the same direction. When the crossings were first installed there was access to platforms 1 and 2 but, as will be seen from the photograph, this facility was removed on electrification in 1904 and only electric trains on the North Tyneside loop could use platforms 1 and 2. *BR*

added, with their own concourse and an entrance from Neville Street; a new booking office was opened on 16 April 1894 but from 2 June 1931 this was replaced by the first mechanised booking office in the country. At that time this was used mainly by passengers on the north bank electrified services, and on the steam services to Sunderland and South Shields. The rapid issuer and multiprinter machines were supplied by the German AEG company and could issue 240 tickets a minute covering some 675 destinations. With the closure of the North Tyne services platforms 1, 2 and 3 became redundant and on 13 March 1983 the tracks were disconnected and the area levelled to form a car park.

The 1894 alterations brought the number of platforms to 15, namely seven bays at the east

Newcastle Central Station Platforms 1939

Plat. No New	Old	Length (ft)	Accommodation (inc. locomotive) 52ft vehicles Non-vestibuled	63ft 6in vehicles Vestibuled
1	(C)	501	8 electric	—
2	(B)	498	9 electric	—
3	(A1)	477	9 electric or 7 coaches	6 coaches
4	(1)	780	13	11
5	(2)	606	9	8
6	(3)	564	9	7
7	(4)	637	9	7
8	(A5)	1,335	24	20
9	(5)	1,023	17	17
10	(8)	978	13	12
11	(A4)	525	9	8
12	(4)	435	7	5
13	(6)	456	7	6
14	(7)	612	9	8
15	(9)	483	8	6

The down main platform, now No 8, was opened on 8 November 1893. The position in 1986 is that platforms 1, 2 and 3 have been removed, and 14 and 15 are not for public use.

end, five at the west end, and three through platforms; although there were two tracks (now only one) between two of the through platforms, Nos 8 and 9, these were classed as sidings and could not be used for trains not stopping at Newcastle, although the only train likely to pass through without stopping was the summer up and down 'Flying Scotsman', following the introduction of the non-stop working in 1928. Consequently the down train was routed via No 8 platform road, and the up train via No 9, although the up train has been known to pass on the lines outside the station.

With the piecemeal development of the station the platforms were numbered hapha-

Top left:
Class A4 No 60001 *Sir Ronald Matthews* arrives from Edinburgh on the up 'Flying Scotsman' on 30 March 1950. The arch of the Tyne (road) Bridge can be seen on the right. *BR*

Centre left:
Mishaps on the busy crossings were rare, but on 19 April 1956 'V2' No 60968 was struck amidships by Fairburn Class 4MT 2-6-4T No 42073 which is out of sight behind the 'V2'. *Ian S. Carr*

Bottom left:
On 3 February 1967 'Jubilee' No 45675 *Hardy* was an unusual visitor and it returned south on the Heaton sidings to Manchester Red Bank newspaper empties; it is seen standing outside Central station with the gable end of the electric signalbox (opened in 1959) projecting through the roof behind. *Ian S. Carr*

zardly until the final extensions took place in the 1890s, and from 7 January 1894 they were renumbered in a series which remains in use to this day, although now of course, there are several blank numbers.

The Author's first recollection of Newcastle Central station is of an occasion in the 1920s when, as a schoolboy, he walked across the lower deck of the High Level Bridge with his father. He insisted on going to the station but the only engine he can remember seeing was Gresley 'A1' Pacific *Merry Hampton* — an engine which he was not to see again for many years. He started using the station regularly in 1943 and also spent many hours on the platforms in his free time. When late in that year he was on a troop train from London to an unknown port of embarkation (which later turned out to be Glasgow) the train stopped to change the crew at Newcastle.

One thing that always struck the Author as unnecessary was the compulsory queueing of passengers outside the barriers for certain trains; the queue often stretched across the concourse and blocked it — a feature never encountered at York. Passengers were not allowed on to the platform until the empty stock arrived from Heaton Carriage Sidings, but even with a ticket it was worth investing 1d for a platform ticket so as to be on the

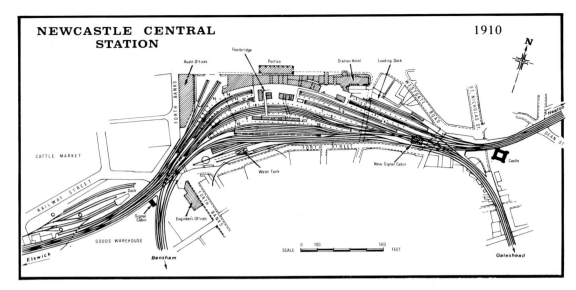

platform before the stock arrived and the queue was allowed through the barriers to dash for the train. Now all that has changed and in 1984 the barriers were removed, making the station 'open' and improving the appearance. The platforms and buildings themselves have changed little; the way through from the main concourse to the east end concourse, between the station buildings and platform 4 has been blocked now that platforms 1, 2 and 3 are no longer available, and at the west end platforms 14 and 15 are not signposted for public use, although the track is still in position.

The booking office in the western entrance from the portico has been closed, as has the information office in the eastern entrance, both replaced by a modern design of travel centre in the concourse, which has its roof supported by rods from vertical metal columns. This has been situated on the site of W. H. Smith's long-established bookstall, which has temporarily been moved to a position across the ends of platforms 11, 12 and 13.

Inside the Travel Centre, with its automatic doors and plate glass frontage, are 14 enquiry and booking positions, although tickets for local stations between York and Berwick (and all ticket sales between 20.30 and 06.00 hours) are handled at three windows at the west end of the structure which is covered in black glass or plastic. The roof of the Travel Centre is surmounted by a large dot matrix arrival and destination indicator. The footbridge is still the same, with a ramp from the concourse, and a ramp to the east and steps to the west down

Top:
Plan of Central station, Newcastle as it was in 1910.

Above:
The interior of the Travel Centre. Note one of the original roof columns in the centre. *BR*

to platform 9. Much of the stonework of the station has been cleaned, both inside and outside the station. There is a well signposted entrance to the Metro on the site of the Hadrian Bar, with escalators between the Metro booking-hall and the platforms under Neville Street.

2 Bridges Across the Tyne

Newcastle is notable for its bridges crossing the Tyne to give access to Gateshead and the south. Three of these are railway bridges, the High Level dating from 1849, the King Edward dating from 1906, and the Queen Elizabeth (Metro) dating from 1981. Other high level railway bridges were planned but were never built.

The problem of crossing the Tyne without descending to the stone arch bridge of 1781 long occupied the minds of engineers and others, and in October 1839 John and Benjamin Green, the Newcastle architects, suggested a high level bridge from near the Castle at Newcastle to Greene's Field at Gateshead. This was intended for pedestrian and road traffic and would have been of laminated timber construction as used by the Greens for railway bridges on the Newcastle & North Shields Railway.

As railways stretched northwards towards the Tyne, with the prospect of a line from London to Edinburgh, the problem increased in importance with the forthcoming need for a railway bridge, and a High Level Bridge Company was formed, still with the Green's design as the leading contender. However, it was suggested that the bridge should be built of more permanent material and the Green's reply was to design a seven-arch stone bridge 90ft above high water, with a 28ft high iron superstructure to carry the railway on its upper deck. This design was referred to George Stephenson in 1842 and the upshot was that Stephenson and George Hudson joined the Management Committee of the High Level Bridge Company, which appointed Robert Stephenson as its consulting engineer.

George Hudson's dedication to establishing an east coast line led to his companies completing the line northwards from Darlington to Gateshead after the Great North of England had failed to build it. To start with, a fine station at Gateshead had to suffice for Newcastle passengers because of the difficulty of bridging the Tyne gorge; however, even before the first train from London reached Gateshead in June 1844 the Newcastle & Darlington Junction Railway had obtained an Act (23 May 1844) which included powers for a bridge across the Tyne. The High Level Bridge Co decided to leave the task of financing and building the bridge to the railways concerned, and as it was considered to be beyond the

Below:
The first railway bridge across the Tyne gorge was Robert Stephenson's High Level Bridge opened in 1849. This had two decks, with the three-track railway on top of the six spans, and the roadway and footways suspended below. It has recently been announced that two tracks are to be removed and a weight restriction applied to road traffic on the lower deck. The low level swing bridge can be seen through the first span, and the top of the Tyne Bridge above the stone parapet. This view was taken from the Gateshead end, on 7 December 1967. *BR*

means of the N&DJ alone an Act of 31 July 1845 transferred the powers to the Newcastle & Berwick Railway, with the proviso that it had to be built jointly with the N&DJ. In addition to the bridge, lines were planned from a junction with the Brandling Junction Railway at Gateshead, from the north end of the bridge to Neville Street in Newcastle, and from the north end of the bridge to join the Newcastle & North Shields Railway at Manors.

Robert Stpehenson and T. E. Harrison (later Engineer of the North Eastern Railway) produced a modified version of the Green's design, crossing the river at the same point, but consisting of six cast iron spans resting on ashlar piers, with masonry approach arches at each end. The three railway tracks were carried on top of the arches, with the roadway suspended below by wrought iron rods.

At that time the river was only 3ft deep but extensive pile driving was necessary and 121 piles each 13in square were required for each of the four river piers; the piles were driven into the river by a Nasmyth steam hammer — the first time this piece of equipment had been used in railway construction. The first pile was sunk on 1 October 1846 and on 12 January 1847 the first brick was laid; the first segment of the first arch — there were four arches to each span — was completed on 10 July 1848 and on 7 June 1849 the rails across the bridge were completed.

To get railway traffic moving, and to assist in the construction of the permanent bridge, a temporary timber bridge with one track was built to one side, using part of the foundations for the permanent bridge, and this was opened on 29 August 1848 when 'A train consisting of nine carriages and a luggage van, and preceded by a powerful engine (weighing 16 tons) was speedily filled by the party assembled at the station. One of the compartments of a first class carriage was occupied by a party of ladies, who were not afraid to cross the dizzy height'. As the train crossed the bridge 'there was a loud discharge of artillery from the castle and other places, and the bells of St Nicholas rang a merry peal'. At Manors Mr Hudson and his friends alighted and proceeded to the Queen's Head 'where a sumptuous meal had been provided for them by the Mayor of Newcastle. Upwards of 700 gentlemen sat down'. Regular traffic over the temporary bridge commenced on 1 September 1848.

One track on the permanent bridge was opened on 15 August 1849, and on 28 September the Royal Train conveying Queen Victoria stopped on the bridge; this is usually taken to be the date of the formal opening, although there was no opening ceremony as such. The removal of the temporary bridge allowed the new bridge to be completed to its full width of 35ft 1in between the parapets on the top (rail) deck.

The six spans are 125ft each, with the piers at 138ft 10in centres. A British Rail survey made in 1963 quotes the height of the rails as 108ft 6in above high water, and by that time the depth of water through spans 3 and 4 was approximately 30ft, after years of dredging. The spans are numbered from 1 to 6 from the Gateshead end, and the structure is officially referred to as Leeds-Newcastle Bridge No 323.

The roadway on the lower deck was completed on 4 February 1850 and a contemporary report states that a ½d toll was being charged for the use of the bridge, although the railway company was allowed to charge 1d. The actual roadway was 20ft 4in wide and was situated between the inner pair of arched girders for the rail deck, with a footway 6ft 2in wide on each side, between the inner and outer girders. Cradles for inspecting the underside of the roadway were installed on each span in 1923, and in 1936 the suspended finials on spans 1 and 6 were removed for reasons unknown.

In a report to the shareholders the cost of the bridge was quoted as £243,096 for the masonry and ironwork, with an additional £113,067 for the viaducts to join the bridge to the Brandling Junction Railway at the Gateshead end, and to the Newcastle & North Shields Railway at the Newcastle end. The cost of the land was said to be £135,000 but the engineer who made the report could not confirm this figure 'which was not in his department'! The weight of iron used was quoted as 5,050 tons.

The contractors for the ironwork were Hawks, Crawshay & Co, Messrs Losh, Wilson & Bell, and Abbott & Co, with the masonry by Rush & Lawton. The work was completed under the supervision of the noted North East engineer T. E. Harrison; at the time he was engineer to the York, Newcastle & Berwick Railway, and later of the North Eastern Railway.

At each end of the brige, at roadway level, there is a metal plate which presumably dates from the completion of the bridge; it reads:

> ENGINEERS
> ROBERT STEPHENSON C.E.
> THOMAS E. HARRISON C.E.
> CONTRACTORS FOR IRONWORK
> HAWKS, CRAWSHAY & SONS
> 1 8 5 0

In 1934 the LNER decided to erect commemorative tablets on various viaducts and bridges in the North Eastern Area, and that on the High Level Bridge was unveiled on Sunday 8 September 1935, with the inscription:

HIGH LEVEL BRIDGE

Opened by

HER MAJESTY QUEEN VICTORIA

28th Sept. 1849

ROBERT STEPHENSON

THOMAS ELLIOT HARRISON

ENGINEERS

The Newcastle & Berwick Act of 1845 included powers to make an extra charge for goods and passenger traffic passing over the High Level Bridge by rail. This was equivalent to an additional three miles at the current rates and it continued to be charged until 1952. The same Act laid down the maximum tolls to be charged over the lower deck of the bridge, ranging from 1d for pedestrians, 3d for a horse and wagon, to 10d for 20 head of cattle; these tolls were abolished from 10 May 1937.

For many years horse buses ran across the High Level Bridge, and an anomaly often remarked upon was that it cost the same to ride or walk over the bridge, namely ½d. This was because the horse buses paid a toll of 4d no matter how many passengers were carried, and thus the fares collected from passengers numbering more than eight was profit for the bus owners. These horse buses ceased running on 12 June 1931.

In 1913 the NER sought powers to run trolley vehicles over the High Level Bridge but failed to get Parliamentary permission. However, after long negotiations, and strengthening of the road deck, trams between Newcastle and Gateshead were introduced on 12 January 1923, with a fare of 1d, of which ½d went to the LNER. The bridge was closed for 28 days to allow a complete renewal of 308yd of the floor carrying the roadway. This was originally carried on 12×12in timbers placed at 3ft 4in between centres, and these were replaced by broad flanged steel beams having a 12in flange top and bottom.

Two grades, Toll Collector and Assistant Toll Collector, were employed on the bridge and both were supplied with summer and winter style uniforms similar to those supplied to Ticket Collectors, but with *TOLL COLLECTOR* in gold on both sides of the collar.

A second railway bridge across the Tyne was planned in 1865 by T. E. Harrison, in connection with the proposed line along the Team Valley south of Gateshead. However, the scheme was never implemented and it was 1906 before the King Edward Bridge was opened, on almost the same site as that chosen in 1865.

Although Newcastle station was a through station this facility was not available to main line trains, which had to enter and leave from the east end. The advent of the King Edward Bridge meant that northbound trains could enter the station at the west end and leave at the east end, and trains from the south terminating at Newcastle could avoid the heavily used High Level Bridge.

After much planning and discussion the tender for the erection of the King Edward Bridge (masonry and steelwork) was awarded to the Cleveland Bridge & Engineering Co Ltd on 13 February 1902 at a figure of £19,882 5s 10d. The bridge consists of four spans of (from the south) 191ft, 300ft, 300ft and 231ft, weighing 1,350 tons, 1,741 tons, 1,741 tons and 950 tons respectively, with masonry arches at both ends. The extra weight of the southern span is accounted for by the fact that the lines diverged to Bensham and Greensfield and so required additional girders.

Top right:

The Metro bridge across the Tyne approaching completion on 26 May 1978. It was named Queen Elizabeth Bridge on 6 November 1981 when HM The Queen travelled to the new interchange station at Heworth. The public opening took place nine days later. *Ian S. Carr*

Centre right:

When opened by the Newcastle & North Shields Railway in 1839, Ouseburn and Willington Dene Viaducts were of laminated timber construction, but both were rebuilt in iron to an unusual design, commencing with Ouseburn in 1868. This is Willington Dene Viaduct with a Newcastle to Tynemouth DMU crossing on 24 July 1980 during the period when the Metro was under construction and BR trains were terminating at Tynemouth. *Ian S. Carr*

Right:

To join the Newcastle & Carlisle route at West Wylam Junction the Scotswood, Newburn & Wylam Railway had to cross the Tyne on this relatively small but imposing bridge. *K. Hoole Collection*

The foundation stone was laid on 29 July 1902 by C. A. Harrison, the nephew of T. E. Harrison. Using caissons, the foundations for the river piers were sunk 69ft below high water level, and the piers themselves were built of granite from Norway. The arches at each end were built of a hard red sandstone obtained from Cove Quarries at Kirkpatrick in Dumfries. When completed the bottom of the girders gave 83ft of headroom above high water level.

Although not completely finished the bridge was formally opened by King Edward VII on 10 July 1906; it was tested using a number of heavy locomotives on 27 September 1906 and regular traffic commenced running over the bridge on 1 October 1906, the first train being the 9.30am from Newcastle to the Great Central line headed by Class Q 4-4-0 No 1930.

The King Edward Bridge was built under the NER Act of 1899, which allowed the NER to charge an additional three miles for all traffic passing over the bridge. This continued under the LNER but was abolished in 1952. When the LNER erected commemorative tablets on certain notable bridges in the North Eastern Area in the 1930s, that on the King Edward Bridge was unveiled on 9 May 1934.

Construction of the bridge resulted in a triangular layout at the south end, all three junctions being controlled by King Edward Bridge signalbox. Trains heading south came off the bridge on a tight right-hand curve, the site of many of the photographs taken by the late R. J. Purves pre-1914. For many years the location remained unchanged, although the lower-quadrant signals were changed to upper-quadrants, but the opening of the new electric box at Gateshead in 1962 changed all that, leaving a bald layout after the demolition of King Edward Bridge box and the removal of the signal gantries. Even the houses in the background of the photographs have disappeared.

One of the smaller and lesser-known bridges across the Tyne is at the western extremity of the Scotswood, Newburn & Wylam line, where it crossed the river to join the Newcastle & Carlisle route at West Wylam Junction. It was originally proposed to cross the river with a girder bridge supported on three river piers, but the possibility of one or more of these penetrating old coal workings and allowing nearby pits to be flooded led to a change of plan.

The new scheme was for a wrought iron free arch, with a suspended deck 240ft long and 30ft wide for the railway tracks; the three ribs

forming the arch, springing from a level 19ft 6in below the rails, had a clear rise of 48ft. The deck was supported from 19 cross girders, which divided it into 20 bays of 12ft, and was 28ft above the summer water level, giving a space for floodwater which in 1771 rose to 23ft above the summer level. The bridge was designed by W. G. Laws, later engineer for the City of Newcastle.

On 6 October 1876 two tank and four tender engines, with a total weight of 333 tons, were used to test the bridge, both while stationary on the bridge and while travelling across it, and the maximum deflection on any of the ribs was 1.2in, with no permanent set. The bridge, of which the Tyne (road) Bridge completed 52 years later is a larger version, now carries a public footpath following the dismantling of the line.

The only other railway bridge to cross the Tyne within the limits of this brief survey is at Scotswood, where the five-span hog-backed girder bridge of 1868 still stands although out of use. This was a replacement for the temporary bridge erected after the original was destroyed by fire on 9 May 1860, whilst undergoing tests for the Board of Trade.

In 1918 planning was going ahead for a proposed new railway bridge across the Tyne, and on 18 September 1919 the NER Estate Agent was authorised to negotiate with Newcastle Corporation for the necessary land. The bridge, situated near St Anthonys, was to carry a line from north of Heaton to Washington. This commenced with north and south connections to the main line at Benton Bank, and crossed the Heaton-Tynemouth line

Top right:
The junctions at the south end of the High Level Bridge and the King Edward Bridge have been favourite photographic viewpoints for at least 80 years. Class Q 4-4-0 No 1877 is seen coming off the High Level Bridge and is about to pass through Gateshead West station to reach the Team Valley route on the 12.20pm Newcastle to York, with its 43min booking over the 44.1 miles between Darlington and York. The photograph was taken on 12 July 1906 before the King Edward Bridge was opened. *LCGB Ken Nunn Collection*

Right:
Sister engine No 1876 is coming off the King Edward Bridge at the south end a few years later, with King Edward Bridge Junction signalbox above the first coach. This was a Carlisle diagram and the engine and men worked Carlisle-Newcastle-York-Newcastle on the first day and Newcastle-Carlisle-Newcastle-Carlisle on the second, putting in 11 hours' duty each day. *R. J. Purves*

east of Walker Gate station; the new bridge was to be constructed across the Tyne gorge at 2½ to 2¾ miles from the commencement of the new line. The line then continued parallel to the Pelaw-Washington route, but about ¼-mile to the east of the 1848 line, finally connecting with it north of Washington station.

Various connections with other lines were planned; north of the Tyne there were north and south connections from the new line near Walker Gate to the Riverside branch between Walker and Carville, where north and south connections were also provided. South of the Tyne there was a lengthy connection from the new line near Wardley, northwards to join the Gateshead to South Shields line near Hebburn and later a proposal for a connection from the south end of the new bridge to join the South Shields to Gateshead line near Felling. Finally, there was a remote connection which ran from the Pontop & South Shields line at Beamish Junction to join the East Coast main line between Birtley and Chester-le-Street.

Planning continued for some years and in April 1922 a price of £35,000 was agreed for the land purchased from Newcastle Corporation. In December 1926 a further stretch of land between the Newcastle Corporation portion and the river was purchased from Lord Northbourne for £36,550, but under the LNER the scheme was allowed to fade away.

Top:
A football special from Newcastle to Middlesbrough also at King Edward Bridge Junction headed by Class 46 No 46011 on 6 September 1983. The box has been demolished and the layout remodelled. The Metro bridge is visible on the left and the arch of the Tyne Bridge can be seen in the distance, above the Traction Maintenance Depot. *Ian S. Carr*

Above:
At King Edward Bridge Junction two tracks drop down on the east side of the Team Valley line, before passing below to reach Dunston; this latter route was used by a local service to Dunston from 1909 to 1926 and is now used by the Newcastle to Carlisle trains, allowing the route over Scotswood Bridge to be closed. In this view Class 40 No 40009 is at the head of the Heaton to Manchester newspaper empties on 29 July 1984. *Ian S. Carr*

3 NER, LNER, and BR Electrics

The North Eastern Railway was fortunate in having at its head a board of directors made up of landed gentry and industrialists, chosen to represent particular areas and interests and to keep their fingers on the pulse of the North-East. As soon as NER interests were threat- the company was in a position to take immediate action. Thus when the electric tramways on Tyneside developed rapidly in the early years of the century, the drastic decrease in local passengers travelling by train required immediate attention, which resulted in the electrification of the lines on the north bank of the river, utilising tracks which were already in existence. The North Eastern was also fortunate in that the northeast area was a pioneer in the widespread distribution of electricity supplies, and the close link between the NER and Messrs Merz & McLellan, the Newcastle-based firm of consultants, proved to be very fruitful. In addition Vincent Raven, the NER Assistant Mechanical Engineer, had a great interest in electric traction, and this combination of circumstances led to the opening of the electric service between Newcastle's New Bridge Street station and Benton on 29 March 1904. The electrified line was rapidly extended so that the Benton to Monkseaton section was opened on 6 June 1904, Monkseaton to Tynemouth on 21 June 1904, and both the Tynemouth to Central Station portion, and the

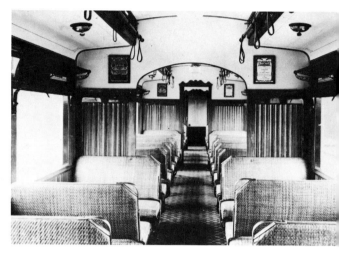

Above:
The interior of No 3519 with its reversible rattan covered seats. *L&GRP (2343)*

Below:
Between 1904 and 1967 a feature of railway operation on Tyneside was the electric service to the coast, inaugurated by the North Eastern Railway using clerestory roofed coaches in a red and cream livery. The vehicles were numbered in the ordinary Coaching Stock list and this is No 3519, a third class motor driving car built in 1909. Note the combined route and destination indicator above the driving cab. *BR*

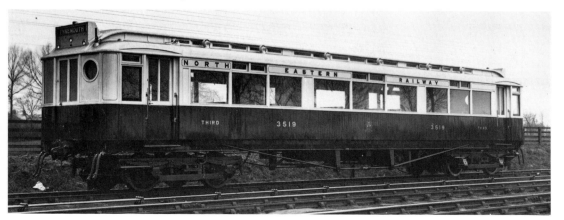

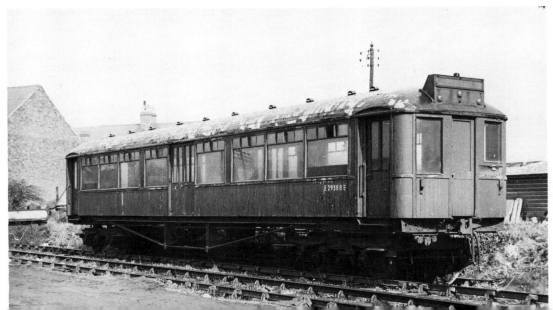

The third motor parcels van No 3525 was built in 1908 and differed in its internal layout from the two 1904 vans. *BR*

Following the fire at Heaton Car Sheds in 1918, 34 replacement vehicles were built with the same numbers as those destroyed, but they differed in having semi-elliptical roofs. When they were built in 1920-22 the colour scheme for the fleet was changed to the standard carriage stock lake, but in 1937 the LNER reverted to the NER red and cream livery, both for the new Metro-Cammell stock and the ex-North Eastern cars refurbished for the South Shields service. These are Nos 23211 and 23212 — a driving trailer third and a motor third respectively. *BR*

In September 1951 No E29388E was converted to a Perambulator Van, with additional doors in the centre of each side and most of the seats removed. In 1960 this car was photographed at South Gosforth awaiting scrapping. *K. Hoole*

Riverside branch on 1 July 1904. The section of the main line between Heaton South Junction and Benton Quarry Junction was electrified on 25 July 1904, together with the southeast and southwest curves; the southwest curve (Benton Quarry Junction to Benton Junction) did not carry a passenger service but eventually proved its worth for empty stock workings to the new Gosforth Car Sheds. The southeast curve (Benton Quarry Junction to Benton East Junction) allowed an express service to be provided from the coastal stations to Newcastle Central without going round by South Gosforth and Jesmond and into New Bridge Street.

The distance between the East Coast main line at Manors and the former Blyth & Tyne station at New Bridge Street was only a few hundred yards but it prevented a truly circular service until the gap was closed from 1 January 1909, when electric trains commenced running between Central and Benton. However, the service soon developed thus:

Central station to:	Via	Mins past the hour
Monkseaton	Wallsend	05
Manors North	Wallsend	20
Tynemouth	Riverside branch	25
Monkseaton	Wallsend	35
Manors North	Wallsend	50

The half-hourly service between Central and Manors North (the station replacing New Bridge Street) took 59min for the journey. Trains arrived at 19 and 49min past the hour, and were due to start their return journey 1min later.

The introduction of circuit running from Central station in 1917 gave a straightforward service at 5 and 35min past the hour via South Gosforth, Backworth and Wallsend, and at 20 and 50min past the hour via Wallsend, Backworth and South Gosforth. Trains between Central and Tynemouth via the Riverside branch ran hourly at 25min past the hour. Journey time was 54min for trains via Backworth and Wallsend, and 53min in the opposite direction. The LNER increased the frequency to trains every 20min via both routes so that there was an electric train leaving Central station every 10min, and with the introduction of the new stock in 1937/38 made a point of advertising 'Trains from Central to Central every 10 minutes alternately via Backworth and via Wallsend from 9.05am to 10.45pm'. In addition there was an express to the coast via Manors North and Backworth (non-stop between Manors and West Monkseaton) every hour on the hour from 9.00am to 11.00pm. These trains then returned as slow trains via the Riverside line and, in the opposite direction, a train from Newcastle via the Riverside branch became an express to Newcastle, running non-stop between West Monkseaton and Manors; this service also ran hourly during the day. When the North Tyneside electric service ceased in June 1967 stopping trains round the circle departed from Central at 20 and 50min past the hour (via Wallsend and Backworth) and at 5 and 35min past the hour via Backworth and Wallsend. During the day there were hourly trains non-stop between West Monkseaton and Manors North, and in the opposite direction.

The NER built all the electric stock at its York Carriage Works, with the electrical equipment supplied and fitted by the contractors British Thomson-Houston. The contract called for an initial fleet of 50 motor cars and 50 trailers, but 58 motor cars (of which two were parcels vans) and 32 trailers were turned out in 1903 and 1904. Between 1905 and 1915 a further 12 motor cars (including a further parcels van) and 23 trailers were built. In the light of experience many of the original cars were modified, either by altering the seating arrangements, by converting from single to double driving control, or by fitting driving equipment in trailer cars, leading to a very complicated history for which there is no space here.

All these vehicles were 55ft 0in over head-stocks and 56ft 6in over body, with a wheelbase of 47ft. They all had a clerestory roof, vertically-panelled matchboard sides and cow-head couplers. The striking livery introduced on the cars was red below the waist and cream above, with the large pattern NER coat-of-arms on each side.

The 34 cars lost in the car sheds fire (Nos 3180/95/97/98, 3204/11/12/17/19/21/25-28/38/41/43/46/49/50/51/68, 3507/08/12/13/18/20/21/24, 3785/88/90/91) were all replaced in 1920-22 by new cars allocated the same numbers, but with elliptical roofs and in the standard NER crimson lake as used for the steam-hauled coaches. When the LNER took over in 1923 the imitation teak livery of the new company was adopted for the fleet of 126 cars, giving a drab and uninviting appearance. To rejuvenate the service after 33 years of

Below left:
In 1937 the LNER put into service 64 articulated twin units and four single cars on the North Tyneside lines. These were built by Metro-Cammell and had rivetted steel bodies and welded underframes. These two outward-bound trains standing in platforms 1 and 2 at Newcastle on 21 February 1967 were routed via Jesmond and Wallsend respectively and would later pass one another travelling in opposite directions.
Ian S. Carr

Bottom:
The LNER stock and the North Eastern refurbished stock were fitted with bucket seats as in No E29304E photographed on 3 March 1967.
Ian S. Carr

Top right:
To replace the North Eastern stock on the South Shields service Eastleigh works built 15 motor seconds and 15 trailer composites in 1954/5, together with a motor luggage van, all being of typical Southern Region design with compartments in place of the traditional open saloons. Motor second No E65317 was photographed at Hebburn. The service to South Shields is now provided by the Metro.
K. Hoole Collection

Below right:
The 1904 electrification included the steeply graded Quayside branch from Trafalgar Yard, Manors, to the riverside. For this duty two electric locomotives were ordered from Brush of Loughborough. As seen here they were originally fitted with bow and shoe pick-up — the bow for use in the yards at top and bottom of the line, and the shoes for use on the climb up through cuttings and tunnels. *K. Hoole Collection*

operation the LNER put into service on 30 July 1937 the first of 64 articulated twin sets (Nos 24145-24272), built by Metro-Cammell Carriage & Wagon Co Ltd, together with two parcels vans (Nos 2424 and 2425), and two Luggage Motor Thirds (Nos 24273 and 24274). These all had steel bodies and underframes and reintroduced the red and cream livery of NER days. As the old stock was displaced some cars were stored because of the international situation and lasted for a few more years, stored as far away as Scarborough. As a wartime measure a change was made to a livery of blue and off-white to render the trains less conspicuous. In 1949 a start was made in painting the cars in BR green with a change to olive green in 1960.

As traffic decreased in the 1960s, with many passengers deserting the trains for the bus and the private car, the reduction in services allowed some vehicles to be withdrawn in 1964, three years before the electric service ceased completely. The last train, which ran on 17 June 1967, was the 18.15 Central to Central via Wallsend, with Motorman E. Higgins at the controls.

As part of the electrification scheme the steeply graded Quayside goods branch was included, and two centre-cab locomotives were built by Brush, with electrical equipment by BTH. These worked from Trafalgar Yard, at the upper end of the branch, down to Quayside Yard, where the wagons with goods for loading into the ships were distributed by a steam locomotive — usually a 'J72' 0-6-0T. Owing to the limited clearances in the tunnels, third-rail

current collection was used for the length of the line, but for safety reasons overhead collection was employed in the yards at the top and bottom of the branch. The latter was originally achieved via a bow mounted on a beam across one end of each locomotive, but this was subsequently replaced by a pantograph mounted centrally on the cab roof. These two locomotives worked very satisfactorily for 59 years, with No 26500 (originally No 1) on duty on 29 February 1964 which was the last day of operation. The load for the electric locomotives on the Quayside branch was 140 tons, compared with 55 tons for a 'J71', 80 tons for a 'J72', and 120 tons for a 'J73'.

To house and service the electric trains a car shed with 12 roads was erected immediately east of the coal stage at Heaton locomotive shed. Unfortunately the building was destroyed by fire on 11 August 1918, and also lost were 34 cars, with many more damaged. Out of the 14 electric sets required each day there were enough vehicles in working order to complete only seven sets, and the other diagrams were covered by steam engines hauling six or seven bogie coaches. Within a week enough damaged cars had been repaired to cover all but three of the electric rosters, and one of those worked only between 4.55pm and 6.25pm.

On 23 October 1918 it was decided not to replace the car shed on the same site, but to look for a new location. That eventually chosen was at Gosforth, out in the country, but by the time the building came to be erected new houses were appearing nearby. All the stock and stores were transferred to the new depot, named South Gosforth, on 30 September 1923 and on the following day it became fully operational. This fine building contains 10 through roads, with two dead-end roads serving the repair shop at the north east corner. In addition to the electric vehicles, BR DMUs were accommodated from 1955, and for these refuelling points and standage roads were provided; but with the withdrawal of the North Tyneside electric services in 1967 only the DMUs remained. However, a new era commenced in the 1970s with the gradual withdrawal of the BR DMU services and their replacement by Tyne & Wear Metro electric cars, which commenced their first public service between Haymarket and Tynemouth on 11 August 1980. Since then the services have been extended, culminating in the opening of the Heworth to South Shields section in March 1984.

Proposals were made in 1908 for the electrification of the Newcastle to South Shields and Sunderland lines, which diverged at Pelaw. However, nothing materialised until 1935, when the LNER announced that it was to electrify the line to South Shields, but not that to Sunderland, which would continue to be worked by steam locomotives. The new service to South Shields came into use on 14 March 1938, running from Gateshead to Pelaw on the course of the Brandling Junction Railway opened in 1839; from Pelaw to Tyne Dock (Harton Junction) was a section opened in 1872 to serve the settlements along the south bank of the Tyne, and for the final two miles to South Shields the course was over a line opened at various times between 1834 and 1879.

To work the new service the LNER refurbished the 34 cars built in 1920/22 to replace a similar number of vehicles lost in the 1918 fire, together with a similar car built in 1928 to replace one lost in a collision. To make an equal number of cars from which to form 18 two-car sets an additional vehicle (No 24465) was built at York in 1938.

In 1954/55 a total of 15 two-car sets were built at Eastleigh for the South Shields service and put into traffic from 10 February 1955; for the first time compartments were used, all NER and LNER stock having had open saloons. A parcels van of similar design (No E68000) was built at Eastleigh in October 1955. Some of the displaced NER vehicles were converted to Perambulator Vans for use on the North Tyneside service at busy times, when the citizens of Newcastle set off for the seaside with their families, the youngest in their prams. Most of the seats were removed from the redundant cars and double doors were fitted in each side to allow easy loading and unloading. In this unique form two of the cars remained in service until the early 1960s.

Top right:
The electric locomotives last worked on 29 February 1964 and were replaced by diesel shunters. Here No 26500 (originally No 1), in green livery with NER and BR crests, stands at Trafalgar Yard with the incline brake van which had extra sanding facilities. The locomotive's successor rests on the right. *Ian S. Carr*

Bottom right:
The electric cars were stabled and maintained at a specially built shed alongside Heaton locomotive depot but this structure was destroyed by fire in 1918, together with 34 cars. This view of the interior dates from around 1905. *K. Hoole Collection*

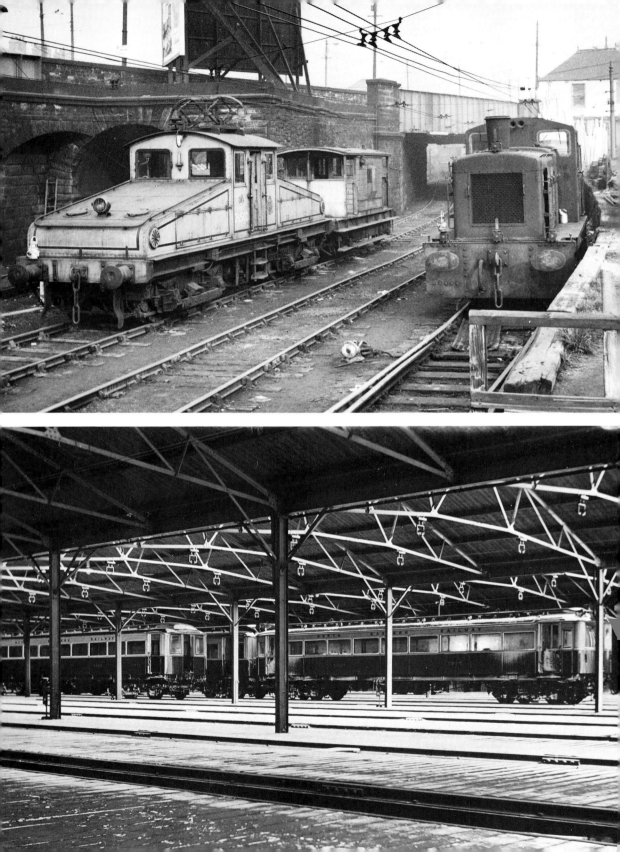

After the electric service was withdrawn from the South Shields line on 7 January 1963, the Eastleigh-built sets were sent to the Southern Region, and the parcels van No E68000 went to the London Midland Region officially on 10 August 1963. Following the closure of the North Tyne lines to electric traction on 17 June 1967 the Metro-Cammell sets were sold to various scrap merchants for cutting up.

The Quayside branch was last worked by an electric locomotive on 29 February 1964 and No 26501 (originally No 2) was sold to a scrap dealer at Choppington in 1966. In 1977 Nos 26500 (originally No 1) eventually found a final resting place at the National Railway Museum at York, where it is currently on display.

Top:
It was decided to build the replacement car sheds at South Gosforth, where a large 10-road shed and a two-road repair shop were opened in 1923. This view is of the west end of the building, with the two Quayside branch electric locomotives in the foreground and Metro-Cammell stock in the background. *Ian S. Carr*

Above:
With the introduction of DMUs on the Middlesbrough and Carlisle services in 1957, South Gosforth took on the maintenance of the DMU fleet based at Newcastle and extra standage was provided on the south side of the sheds. This 1957 view shows the new tracks and a newly delivered Metro-Cammell four-car set. *K. Hoole*

4 Train Services

From the day in 1844 when the first train ran through from London to Gateshead, the service to and from the capital has been the most important to Newcastle and Tyneside. The journey time has been reduced over the years, the stock has been improved out of all recognition, and the locomotive workings have been extended; now, instead of the once invariable engine changes at Grantham, York and Newcastle the IC125 sets work between London and Aberdeen throughout, on a daily basis. The first extended engine working on the main line commenced soon after the Grouping, when North Eastern Atlantics from Gateshead shed began working from Newcastle to Grantham, followed in 1927 by London to Newcastle non-stop, and in 1928 by London to Edinburgh without a stop. Through engine workings reduced the time spent at stations, improved the overall time and, perhaps more importantly, allowed more mileage to be obtained from a locomotive in its working day. Thus to some extent train services have followed locomotive development, although in the LNER and BR periods the use of large engines such as 'D49s' in place of a 'D17' 4-4-0, a 'B1' 4-6-0 instead of a 'D20' 4-4-0, or a 'V1' 2-6-2T in place of a 'G5' 0-4-4T must have nullified much of the economy.

The introduction of the East Coast Joint Stock in 1861 was another factor which improved the service provided for the travelling public. Originally coaches were restricted to their own line, but the coaches built and operated jointly by the Great Northern, North Eastern and North British companies obviated the bane of many travellers — the necessity to change trains! This became a thing of the past as far as travellers between London and Edinburgh were concerned, it only being necessary to change trains to reach destinations off the main line. However, the use of through coaches, where a coach and its passengers were transferred from one train to another at junction stations, was another facility appreciated by the travelling public, although at Newcastle the through coaches were usually only passing through, commencing or terminating there, and passengers on main line trains had to change for all destinations on the branches radiating from Newcastle.

Below:
The East Coast main line was for many years the main target for train photographers in the North-East and it happened that lineside access was easier south of Gateshead than north of Newcastle. Consequently various well-known photographers spent time at Low Fell from about 1900. Class S1 4-6-0 No 2115 is at the head of a down express at Low Fell. *K. Hoole Collection*

When there were sufficient passengers for one destination, or to stations en route to that destination, then a through train was introduced. From Newcastle, at one time or another, it was possible to reach Bournemouth, Southampton, Liverpool, Scarborough, Glasgow and many other towns and cities in through trains, with the stock provided by, for example, the Great Western, London & North Western, Lancashire & Yorkshire, London & South Western and Great Central Railways, often with restaurant car facilities. However, in no case did the originating company's engines

work north of York on trains from the south, and neither did North British engines work south of Berwick. Thus the working arrangements known as 'Running Powers' were not invoked and the through trains were usually arranged by personal discussions between the respective general managers, leading to an agreement being signed by both parties.

After the London service, that between Newcastle, Manchester and Liverpool was probably the best known and the longest established. This was not worked by Joint stock, but the North Eastern and Lancashire & Yorkshire companies provided trains for the Normanton route and a similar arrangement existed with the London & North Western regarding the Leeds route. Thus it was possible to see L&Y and LNWR trains in Newcastle on a daily basis thoughout the year. The L&Y trains ran via York and Darlington, and the LNWR trains usually travelled via Harrogate, Northallerton and Sunderland, although changes took place in LNER days and some trains via Leeds and Harrogate used the main line north of Northallerton. Also in LNER days the L&Y route trains made an out-and-home journey daily, but the LNWR route working was slightly more complicated; the Newcastle-based set of coaches worked to Liverpool on the first day, from Liverpool to Newcastle and back on the second, and from Liverpool to Newcastle on the third.

As Newcastle Central handled hundreds of trains a day over a period of 135 years it is impossible to describe all the changes that have taken place in the train services. However copies of Bradshaw's *Monthly Railway and Steam Navigation Guide* and similar publications are available at various centres for serious students of train services, and the

Top left:
'R1' 4-4-0 No 1244 passes Low Fell station on an up express. *R. J. Purves*

Centre left:
Class C 0-6-0 No 56 at Low Fell, probably on a Durham slow train, with a North Eastern fish wagon at the usual position at the front of the train giving the passengers a smell of the sea! *W. Rogerson*

Bottom left:
Trains from Low Fell Yard or even Forth Goods joined the main line at Low Fell but could run on the slow lines to Ouston Junction, south of which there were only two tracks. This wartime view, taken on 19 May 1940, is of Class C7/2 No 732 on an up goods. *W. B. Greenfield*

Below:
Low Fell station closed to passengers on 7 April 1952 but the signalbox remained open until 1963 and was demolished later that year. Class V2 No 60961 passes the site of the station on an up express. Note that the upper-quadrant arms for the train are mounted on the same post as the lower-quadrant arm in the view of No 1244 some 50 years earlier. *E. E. Smith*

Public Record Office at Kew has the file of North Eastern Railway timetables, which were removed from the former NER Head Offices at York when the BRB Historical Records organisation was disbanded in the 1970s.

In 1870 the North Eastern public timetable was a 54 page booklet, measuring 6¼in × 9¾in, and the price was 2d; but soon afterwards (at least by the July 1872 issue) it had changed its size to a 7½in × 11¾in format, which remained standard until some time during World War 1; this sold for 1d. There was also a pocket timetable 4in × 7¾in which also cost 1d. Following World War 1, a 5in × 6½in format was adopted but it was priced at 6d, although with the succeeding LNER timetable the price was reduced to 1d.

Bradshaw's guide for July 1847 (by which time the Newcastle & Carlisle Railway had reached its new terminus at Forth) listed departures for Carlisle at 6.00am, 9.00am, 11.00am, 1.45pm, 4.00pm and 6.45pm, all stopping at every station and taking at least 3¼hr for the journey, including the 11.00am mail train. The two trains in both directions on Sundays led to strong condemnation from leading churchmen and others. The fare from Newcastle to Carlisle was first class 11s, second class 8s 6d, and third class 5s.

In the same issue, the fastest train shown from London was the 9.25am from Euston Square, due in Newcastle at 6.05pm, but the mail train at 9.00pm from London did not reach Newcastle until 10.00am the next

morning. Of course at that period the trains actually terminated at Gateshead as the High Level Bridge had not yet been built, and it is not made clear if the Newcastle arrival time quoted in the tables applies to the Gateshead terminus, or if it refers to the arrival of the cross-river ferry at Newcastle. Fares from Newcastle to York were first class 20s, second class 14s, and third class 9s.

The Newcastle to Berwick service was dealt with in a mere four lines, with no details of the intermediate stations, but merely gave the departure time from Newcastle to Berwick (Tweedmouth station) at 7.30 and 10.30am, and 2.30, 6.15 and 11.30pm.

Fares from Newcastle to Tweedmouth were first class 13s 6d, second class 8s 6d, and third class 5s 6d. From the Gateshead, Shields and Wearmouth table it appears that the trains started at the same time from the three termini, namely at 5.30am, and then ran hourly from 8.00am to 9.00pm.

By 1872 the Carlisle line trains were still taking some three hours for the journey, although, by omitting to call at five stations, the 10.15am from Newcastle reached Carlisle at 12.55pm. The North British train leaving Newcastle at 6.45am only picked up passengers for the Border Counties line from stations to Hexham, but this condition did not apply to the North British trains at 11.40am and 4.30pm, the only restriction being that return tickets were not available between Newcastle and Hexham on these trains.

Above left:
Ouston Junction, with the Consett line curving away over the rear of the IC125 set forming the 07.45 Kings Cross to Edinburgh. The bridge abutments in the foreground are the remains of a wagonway bridge. *Ian S. Carr*

Above:
Class D17/1 No 1621, seen from the overtrack signalbox south of Manors station, was on an Alnwick-Alnmouth-Newcastle train, when the sets were at an intermediate stage, with two

Gresley vestibuled coaches in the centre and a NER brake-third at each end, due to the Gresley brakes being late in delivery. The engine is now preserved, resplendent in NER green, in the National Railway Museum at York but the signalbox was destroyed by fire on 13 June 1943. *W. B. Greenfield*

Below:
Gresley 'A3' Pacific No 60080 *Dick Turpin* passing Manors East with the 10.42 relief from Newcastle to Glasgow on 1 August 1964. *Ian S. Carr*

Above:
The changing East Coast locomotive scene — and the changing Newcastle skyline! 'Deltic' No 55015 *Tulyar* heads the 08.10 Newcastle to Berwick train on 3 July 1979. *Ian S. Carr*

Below:
Manors North station on the 1909 link between the old Blyth & Tyne station at New Bridge Street and the East Coast main line, with the diverted 12.20 Edinburgh to King's Cross on 6 June 1976. The engine is 'Deltic' No 55001 *St Paddy.* *Ian S. Carr*

Above right:
In the 1930s local services beyond the electric lines were usually worked by 'A5' and 'A8' 4-6-2Ts, 'V1' 2-6-2Ts, or 'G5' 0-4-4Ts, but a stranger in use on a train from Newbiggin was No 693 of Class A6, seen passing Argyle Street signalbox. The overhead wires in the foreground are for the Quayside electric locomotives operating in Trafalgar Yard, which is on the right. *W. B. Greenfield*

The 10.00am from King's Cross had been introduced by 1872 and, stopping only at Peterborough, Grantham and York, it was into Newcastle at 4.25pm and Edinburgh at 7.30pm. This included a 25min meal halt at York and in the North Eastern timetable it was shown as 'Scotch Express'. The Newcastle to London fare was now first class 48s 1d; second class 36s 4d, and Government 22s 7d. Services on branches around Newcastle had greatly increased in frequency, with 25 trains to Tynemouth, 17 to Sunderland, and 18 to South Shields.

By the turn of the century the 'Scotch Express' had gained an hour and was into Edinburgh at 6.30pm. The Tynemouth loop had been created by the short junction line at Tynemouth, and the Riverside branch was in use, although one condition imposed on Sundays was that passengers travelling from Heaton and Walker Gate to Willington Quay had to detrain at Wallsend and walk to nearby Carville station to join a Riverside branch train to their destination. Another was that passengers from the Riverside line wishing to travel to Howdon had to detrain at nearby Willington Quay station and walk from there!

The final North Eastern public timetable, which ran to 116 pages, included an advertisement for the 1,000 mile tickets at £9 9s, enabling the purchaser, his family, guests or employees to travel first class at only ½d per mile more than the third class fare. The 10.00am from Kings Cross was into Newcastle at 3.42pm, but the arrival time at Edinburgh was still 6.30pm. The electric trains via the coast required a full page for the service in one direction, and there were eight steam trains to Morpeth starting from Manors North and sharing the electric lines as far as Backworth. The Newcastle to Carlisle table included the 12.40am non-stop, with a through coach to Stranraer and a connection to the steamer for Larne; this had a timing of 87min between Newcastle and Carlisle, but the fastest day time train at 1.20pm from Central was allowed 104min with four stops. In the same table there were 15 trains from Newcastle terminating at Hexham.

In 1927 a regular non-stop run between London and Newcastle was introduced, leaving King's Cross at 9.50am, in advance of the 'Flying Scotsman', and due in Newcastle at 3.20pm. This paved the way for a London to Edinburgh non-stop working and for the first time, from 1 May 1928, the up and down 'Flying Scotsman' trains passed through Newcastle without stopping.

Although a general acceleration of services took place in 1932, it was the introduction of the 'Silver Jubilee' streamlined locomotives and train in 1935 that brought Newcastle into the high-speed age. However, the four-hour timing over the 268 miles to Kings Cross looks very slow when compared with today's 2hr 52min for the up 'Flying Scotsman'. Also the

'Silver Jubilee' was the only train of the day to run at that speed, leaving Newcastle at 10.00am and Kings Cross at 5.30pm, with a stop at Darlington in both directions. Now it is difficult to imagine the stir that was created by the silver engines built at Doncaster, and the set of coaches to go with them, which created such an impression on the general public that crowds turned out to see them on their trial runs, and for some time after the regular service had commenced.

In 1937 the second streamlined train was put into service in the shape of the 'Coronation', leaving Kings Cross at 4.00pm and Edinburgh at 4.30pm and thus requiring two sets of coaches. On the down journey the train stopped only at York, but on the up run a stop was made at Newcastle from 6.30 to 6.33pm, leaving 237min to reach Kings Cross. However, a stop at Newcastle was introduced on the down working from March 1938.

After World War 2 an early attempt to capture the Newcastle to London traffic led to the introduction in 1948 of the 'Tees-Tyne Pullman', leaving Newcastle at 9.00am and taking 5hr 16min for the journey to London! Pullman trains serving Newcastle were not new as the 'Harrogate Pullman', introduced in 1923, terminated at Newcastle for the first two years, before being extended to Edinburgh and eventually becoming the 'Queen of Scots', also revived after World War 2.

Throughout the 1930s Tyneside saw various types of diesel locomotive and rail car as Armstrong Whitworth & Co attempted to interest the British main line railway companies in diesel traction, but Armstrong Whitworth's greatest success was overseas. Nevertheless diesel-electric main line and shunting locomotives made their appearance on Tyneside, and the three railcars *Tyneside Venturer*, *Lady Hamilton* and *Northumbrian* were to be seen on demonstration runs to and from Central station. On 25 September 1933 the Armstrong Whitworth railbus (with body by Park Royal Coachworks Ltd) was put into regular service in the area.

However, World War 2 put a stop to any further development and it was not until 1955 that the first Derby-built diesel multiple unit reached Newcastle and was based at South Gosforth electric car sheds. These Derby cars were of typical British appearance, with vertical ends and little customer appeal apart from their cleanliness and the novelty of being able to look over the driver's shoulder. Eventually all the local services, together with those to Carlisle and Middlesbrough, were

operated with DMUs, including the replacements for the North and South Tyneside electric services.

Saturday 21 June 1958 saw the appearance of the first main line diesel locomotive when Type 4 No D201 worked from London to Newcastle on the down 'Flying Scotsman' (arriving at 3.07pm) and returned on the 5.05pm from Newcastle. This quick turn-round of less than 2hr would have been considered impossible in steam days but it was accomplished on numerous occasions thereafter when a diesel failed to appear! The arrival of the 'Deltics' in 1961 — Nos D9002/5/8/11/14/17 were allocated to Gateshead shed — meant that speed was at last a saleable commodity, but it also meant the end of the Gresley Pacifics, which had served the East Coast main line for 40 years. The change from steam to diesel traction on the non-stop 'Elizabethan' eliminated the gangway connection between train and locomotive and thus the ability to carry out crew changes without stopping. A stop at Newcastle for this purpose was therefore included in the train working procedure, with no facility for the joining or leaving of the train by passengers.

The prototype IC125 made trial runs to Newcastle in 1973, but it was 1978 before the production series went into regular service, commencing with the 07.45 Kings Cross to Edinburgh and the 15.00 return. However, the

Above:
A Swindon-built cross-country DMU on a return excursion from Nottingham loading at Whitley Bay on 26 August 1973. *Ian S. Carr*

Below:
New Class 140 DMU No 140 001 pauses at Gateshead East (closed later the same month) on a Newcastle to Sunderland working on 4 November 1981. The tracks for the High Street to Greensfield line are carried on the girder bridge on the right.
Ian S. Carr

Left:
A street scene at South Shields as a DMU to Newcastle crosses King Street bridge on 20 April 1981. Metro trains now terminate at a platform which crosses the bridge some 100yd short of the NER terminus, where the station buildings still exist. *Ian S. Carr*

inability to 'strengthen' a train has often led to passengers having to stand for long distances, and a standing passenger is virtually a lost passenger. He will go by coach or car next time!

Now electrification is in view again! It has already been announced that this will do little to increase speeds and reduce timings, but will give improved efficiency and economy. It comes, of course, 65 years after the NER had planned the electrification of the York to Newcastle section of the main line, in that far-off postwar period when Grouping was only a possibility and the LNER had not been formed.

Fortunately nothing further has been heard of Dr Beeching's proposal to close the main line between Newcastle and Edinburgh, which would have meant passengers going across to Carlisle before heading for Edinburgh and paying for the extra mileage involved. Admittedly little traffic is generated on the 124 miles between Newcastle and Edinburgh, but it is the service that can now be provided between London and Eastern Scotland that attracts the passengers.

In steam days the hourly Newcastle to Middlesbrough service, latterly in the hands of 'V1' and 'V3' 2-6-2T engines, was regular, reliable, and reasonably quick; on the Carlisle line the 'D49' 4-4-0s from Gateshead shed also did well. Certainly changes in travelling habits, industrial depression and the private car have all had an effect on these services, and they are now run half-heartedly, with ageing DMU sets calling at unattractive stations. It is to be hoped that the alterations and improvements currently taking place at Newcastle Central have some effect, especially now that it is possible to travel to most parts of Tyneside between Newcastle and the coast, on both sides of the river, with direct access from the Central station concourse to the Metro system.

On both sides of the Tyne a number of alternative routes were available in the event of a blockage by accident or engineering works. The East Coast main line was, of course, the most important artery and in the event of a stoppage on the Team Valley route through Birtley the old main line from Ferryhill, through Leamside, Penshaw, Washington, Pelaw and Gateshead was extensively used at one time, but its severe reduction in status (and maintenance) means that it now sees less use. If necessary trains could travel via Durham and join the old main line at Leamside, but the usual method was to run a shuttle service between Durham and Leamside to connect with diverted up and down main line trains. This took place even after Leamside station had been closed to regular passenger traffic.

Further north it was possible to diverge from the Team Valley route at Low Fell, and run via Norwood Junction, Scotswood, and into Central station via the Newcastle & Carlisle line, or to use Bensham Curve, pass below the main line, and climb to King Edward Bridge Junction via what were (at that time) goods lines. Now, of course, the Newcastle to Carlisle trains use that route to reach Blaydon, serving the re-opened station at Dunston on the way.

Blockage of either the High Level Bridge or the King Edward Bridge could cause complications, but traffic could be kept on the move thanks to the two bridges and the triangular junctions at the south end of both of them; if the High Level Bridge was blocked the South Shields electric trains could not reach Central station and a steam service had to be substituted, and if the King Edward Bridge was blocked the East Coast trains had to use the High Level Bridge, which meant reversing in Central station. At times, trains from Newcastle to the south via Sunderland and Stockton were unable to use the direct route to Sunderland, and from Pelaw took the South Shields line as far as Harton Junction (near Tyne Dock station) where they reversed and rejoined their correct route at Tile Shed Junction, north of Sunderland.

On the north bank of the Tyne one route often used when the main line was blocked between Manors and Forest Hall was via Jesmond and South Gosforth, taking the World War 2 curve at Benton to rejoin the main line at Benton North Junction. This curve was originally authorised in 1900, and although signals controlling access to the line were erected at the east end of Benton station it was not completed until 40 years later! However, this route has become a casualty of progress in the form of the Metro system; the only alternative route to remain is that which runs via the main line to Benton Quarry Junction, then on the realigned south-east curve, under the Metro, continuing on a single line on the north side of the Metro tracks as far as Backworth (where the station has completely vanished), and finally taking the curve to what was once Earsdon Junction to join the former Blyth & Tyne route to Bedlington and Morpeth. At Morpeth a new east to north curve allows the main line to the north to be gained without the need to reverse in Morpeth station, which for so long proved a hindrance to traffic between Scotland and coastal stations such as Monkseaton and Whitley Bay. This route proved of great importance when the Morpeth derailment occurred in June 1984.

Blockages on the main line further north — such as when the Penmanshiel Tunnel collapsed, for instance — have sent Edinburgh to Newcastle trains round via Carlisle.

Significant operational flexibility has been possible at Newcastle Central owing to the existence of the two bridges and the junctions immediately south of them. Recall of the occasion when two empty stock trains from Heaton carriage sidings were despatched in the wrong order provides a good illustration. The first train to arrive at Central was due to form a departure from the same platform as the second, and to correct matters the first train was routed on to the goods lines behind the station and held there, allowing the second train to reach its correct platform and depart as booked. There was no need for any complicated movements to get the first train into its platform; all that was necessary was

for it to run via King Edward Bridge, Gateshead West and High Level Bridge for it to arrive in the platform as if nothing had happened!

No mention has been made of the intensive freight and mineral traffic which once worked around Newcastle and, of course, such trains appeared only in the Working Timetable issued to staff. However there were many workings which depended on the arrival or departure of ships in the river, on the amount of coal raised at certain pits, on material required at shipyards and works, on the despatch of dead locomotives from Stephenson's or Hawthorn's works, or on occasional out-of-gauge loads. The locomotives to work these were ordered as required through the control; a Freight Train Control was established at Newcastle on 3 December 1917.

An invaluable guide to staff at Central station was the Steam Train Working booklet (which also included the electric trains on the South Shields branch but not those on the Tynemouth lines). This gave the time of arrival and departure of every train, (empty or loaded) using Central station, the platform at which it arrived or departed, the next working of the engine which brought in the train and the previous working of the engine that took it out, together with the Diagram Number of the engine and crew. From this it was possible to tell at which shed the engine was stationed, if it was a North Eastern Area engine. 'Foreign' engines were denoted by SA (Southern Area) or SSA (Southern Scottish Area), obviously most of the SA engines being from King's Cross and the SSA engines from Haymarket.

Accommodation for coaching stock was always a problem. For instance, in 1939 the Liverpool train due at 3.16pm was worked empty to Pelaw at 3.36pm by a Heaton engine and brought back to Central at 4.40pm by the same engine, ready to depart for Liverpool at 5.00pm. The Bristol mail set which arrived at 6.00am was worked out to Low Fell at 6.30am and stood there until returned to Central at 6.35pm to form the 7.10pm departure.

Top right:
Trains to and from Tyne Commission Quay had to reverse at Percy Main North, and for many years the through coaches and trains from King's Cross were worked by 'A5' 4-6-2Ts, and later 'V1' and 'V3' 2-6-2Ts. Here V1 No 67651 is seen. *E. E. Smith*

Bottom right:
'Peak' No D170 at Tyne Commission Quay on 27 April 1969, forming the 14.50 to Newcastle and King's Cross. *Ian S. Carr*

Above:
Eventually passengers had to change at Newcastle and join a DMU for the journey to the Quay station. This is the last regular passenger train from Tyne Commission Quay to Newcastle arriving at Percy Main North, where it reversed, on 2 May 1970 with 'The Norseman' headboard. The rail service was replaced by buses. *Ian S. Carr*

Below:
Thankfully mishaps and accidents on our railway system are remarkably rare. This minor incident occurred at Newcastle on 10 May 1977 when 'Deltic' No 55013 *The Black Watch* was derailed entering Platform 9 with the 08.00 Edinburgh to King's Cross. Here repair work to the track is in progress following the rerailing operations. *Ian S. Carr*

5 Branch Lines

Although the Stanhope & Tyne Railroad built a line from Stanhope to South Shields, through Consett, much of the line was on inclines and was not suitable for passenger traffic. It was not until the NER built a line following roughly the same route, that could be worked by locomotives, that a regular passenger service was introduced between Newcastle, Birtley, Consett and Blackhill in 1896.

The branch diverged from the main line at Ouston Junction, south of Birtley, and joined the former Stanhope & Tyne route from South Sheilds at South Pelaw. The S&T route continued to Stella Gill and the inclines, but the new line turned off almost immediately and started the long climb, much of it on a gradient of 1 in 50, through Pelton, Beamish, Shield Row (renamed West Stanley in 1934), Annfield Plain and Leadgate, to reach Consett at a level 830ft higher than that where it left the Team Valley line.

This was an area honeycombed with early coal workings; some of the larger pits at one time sent their coal to the Tyne on early wagonways, but the largest industrial development was the formation of the Derwent Iron Co in 1840, which became the Derwent & Consett Iron Co in 1858, and the Consett Iron Co in 1864. As early as the 1860s the company had acquired a share in ore deposits in Spain and henceforward largely relied on imported ores, eventually leading to the postwar building of the ore terminal at Tyne Dock, and the introduction in 1951 of the braked ore trains. At first these trains were worked by WD 'Austerity' 2-8-0 and 'Q7' 0-8-0 engines, but

Below:

The line to Carlisle was the most important branch of those radiating from Newcastle, with hourly stopping trains to Hexham from 8.50am to 9.50pm. Class G5 No 1795, for long a Blaydon engine, was photographed leaving platform 12 at Newcastle in 1946, in its wartime livery of unlined black with the letters 'NE' in place of 'LNER'. *K. Hoole Collection*

became much better known with the introduction of the BR Standard Class 9F 2-10-0 locomotives.

The passenger service on the line was withdrawn on 23 May 1955, but the mineral traffic continued until the demise of the Consett Ironworks in September 1980.

The first section of the Newcastle & Carlisle Railway was opened to passengers in 1835, but it was 1 March 1837 before the line reached the Redheugh terminus at Gateshead, and exactly 10 years later that it reached the Forth terminus at Newcastle. When the line reached Central station on 1 January 1851 it was still owned by the independent Newcastle & Carlisle company and it was 1862 before it was taken over by the North Eastern.

In addition to the trains covering the 60 miles to Carlisle, there was a busy local service between Newcastle and Hexham, serving 10 intermediate stations in the 20¾ miles, although Mickley disappeared from the time-table in 1915. The section between Newcastle and Hexham was also served by the North British trains heading for the Border Counties line, and at one time the 4.27pm from Newcastle ran as a through train to Edinburgh, where it was due at 9.26pm. Over the North Eastern part of its journey it was classed as an express! The Border Counties line trains were withdrawn on 15 October 1956.

For many years the Newcastle-Hexham service was worked by the useful Class G5 0-4-4Ts from Hexham and Blaydon sheds, and it was not until the end of steam in the North East was looming that larger engines in the shape of 'V1' and 'V3' 2-6-2Ts were stationed at Hexham. In addition, Hexham was the favourite destination for the Armstrong Whitworth diesel-electric railcars when on trial and demonstration runs from the maker's works at Scotswood, whether working singly or in pairs. Other strangers on the line included London & North Western engines on excursions to Newcastle Races, held on the Town Moor. The earliest known example appeared around 1890, when Special 'DX' 0-6-0 No 1723 (built in 1868) was noted, and on 25 June 1913, 0-6-0 No 318 from Workington shed ran into the buffers at Central station whilst working an excursion from Whitehaven.

The service from Newcastle to Carlisle currently consists of 10 trains daily and five on Sundays; of these the 09.40 from Newcastle stops only at Hexham and Haltwhistle, and the 15.38 from Newcastle at Wylam, Prudhoe, Hexham and Haltwhistle; all the others stop at every station. There are 16 trains from Newcastle to Hexham between 05.53 and 23.42 each weekday (14 on Saturdays), and two Monday-to-Friday trains between Newcastle

and Haltwhistle. Four trains from Newcastle terminate at Hexham on Sundays.

Since 4 October 1982 Newcastle to Carlisle trains have been diverted via Dunston and the section between Scotswood and Blaydon has been closed. However, there is still a single line over the 2 miles 66 chains from the west end of Newcastle Central to Scotswood, and thence over the Scotswood, Newburn & Wylam line to Newburn.

The Newcastle & North Shields Railway was opened on 22 June 1839, and extended at its eastern end to Tynemouth in 1847. The Newcastle terminus was at Manors, where there was a small station slightly to the west of the present one. Following the opening of the temporary High Level Bridge, and before the Central station was ready, trains from the south terminated at Manors.

The early history of the various stations at Manors is confused. With the opening of Newcastle Central in 1850, Manors station was probably resited to serve the Newcastle to Berwick trains, but it was not until the 1880s

Left:

In the postwar period 'B1' 4-6-0s took over most of the workings to Carlisle. On 12 September 1956 No 61012 *Puku* is ready to depart from platform 14 with the 4.20pm to Carlisle. *Ian S. Carr*

Below:

Coming off the Carlisle line at the west end of Newcastle Central is 'Deltic' No 9017 *The Durham Light Infantry* on the 10.00 (retimed to 09.00) from Edinburgh diverted via Carlisle because of engineering works at Dunbar. The building in the background is Forth Goods station, and the date 23 July 1972. *Ian S. Carr*

Above and top:
Until 1911 Blaydon was served by a cramped and inconvenient station (top). A new station was opened at Blaydon in 1911 (above), but 66 years later it was described as 'nasty and derelict' and British Rail admitted that it was 'the eyesore of all eyesores', with peeling noticeboards and the uncleared remains of a fire that had occurred three years previously. *K. Hoole Collection/J. F. Mallon*

that any main line trains are listed as stopping — and then only in the up direction — probably as a result of the quadrupling between Manors and Heaton from 1 April 1887, and the opening of a new Manors station on 13 June 1887.

When the link between Manors and New Bridge Street was opened on 1 January 1909 the main line station was renamed Manors East and the adjacent station, with two through platforms and three bays, was named Manors North. According to British Rail records the suffixes East and North were

dropped from February 1969, but they last appeared in the public timetable in 1947. Manors North closed on 23 January 1978 because of the construction of the Metro.

To the east of Gateshead the Brandling Junction Railway operated services from its Oakwellgate terminus to South Shields and Monkwearmouth, and between Monkwearmouth and South Shields; these commenced on 5 September 1839, but in the following year the section between Cleadon Lane Junction (later

Above right:
Class 40 No D365 heads east through Blaydon station on an engineer's train from How Mill to Tyne Yard. Minutes later the locomotive caught fire at Scotswood causing delay to the East Coast expresses diverted via Carlisle on 23 July 1972. *Ian S. Carr*

Below right:
The diverted 13.35 (retimed to 12.40) Edinburgh-King's Cross approaches Blaydon behind Class 47 No 1508, on 23 July 1972. *Ian S. Carr*

Left:
**Travelling in the opposite direction 'Deltic'
No 9020 *Nimbus* passes Blaydon on the diverted
10.00 from King's Cross, again on 23 July 1972.**
Ian S. Carr

Top left:
**The Riverside branch carried passengers and
freight to the shipyards on the north bank of the
Tyne, but the passenger service was withdrawn on
23 July 1973, and although the line still carries
some freight traffic it cannot be used as a through
route. This view shows the 08.23 Tynemouth-
Newcastle leaving Carville and passing the
entrance to the Swan Hunter Wallsend shipyard.**
Ian S. Carr

Above:
**Carville station on the Riverside branch with the
final Saturday 12.00 Newcastle-West Monkseaton
on 3 October 1970. Note the extra tall signalbox.**
Ian S. Carr

Above right:
**Longbenton station on the North Tyneside loop
was opened on 14 July 1947.** *Ian S. Carr*

Tile Shed Junction) and Harton Junction, used
by the Monkwearmouth to South Shields
trains, was closed and the traffic routed via
Brockley Whins (renamed Boldon Colliery from
1 March 1926). However, the direct line for
Monkwearmouth to South Shields trains was
relaid in 1867 and used until 14 June 1965.

With the introduction of through trains
between London and Gateshead in 1844 the
section between Brockley Whins and Gateshead became part of the East Coast main line,
although after the opening of the Washington
to Pelaw cut-off in 1850 their use of the
Brandling Junction line was restricted to the
section from Pelaw to Gateshead.

On 1 March 1872 the North Eastern opened a
line from Pelaw to Tyne Dock to serve the
industrial and residential development along
the south bank of the Tyne; the line followed
the course of the river and was electrified by
the LNER in 1938. British Rail passenger
trains were withdrawn from the line from
1 June 1981 in preparation for the introduction
of Metro services on tracks which now climb
from Pelaw to cross the Sunderland line; still
running alongside, however, is the 4¼ mile
long BR single line from Pelaw to Simonside
wagon works. Approaching South Shields the
Metro now takes a more easterly route to serve
the Chichester area of the town, before
terminating at a new station in South Shields.

British Rail trains can still reach Pelaw from Newcastle over separate metals, with the main service continuing to Sunderland, Hartlepool, Stockton and Middlesbrough, including one IC125 in both directions between Newcastle and King's Cross, which reverses at Middlesbrough.

Another branch line which carried a service from Newcastle was actually part of the original East Coast main line, from Pelaw via Washington and Fencehouses to Leamside, with some trains continuing to Durham and others to Ferryhill. In the 1930s those that terminated at Ferryhill were worked by steam railcars but one long-established working, the 5.07pm from Newcastle, was locomotive-worked and continued on to York as did two trains on Sundays.

From 28 July 1941 the two stations at Shincliffe and Sherburn Colliery were closed and the Leamside to Ferryhill section lost its regular passenger service. At the northern end one train in each direction continued to run from Newcastle to Usworth and Washington, but these were withdrawn from 9 September 1963, leaving only the 4.35am from Newcastle to Durham, which continued until 4 May 1964. Passenger trains have been seen many times since then, however, as the Ferryhill to Pelaw section is still available for through running in an emergency (with a maximum permitted speed of 60mph) although there are numerous restrictions of 40mph and less. There is a 1 mile 9 chain length of single line across the Victoria Bridge over the Wear.

The Blyth & Tyne was primarily a coal-carrying line between the Blyth area and the Tyne. It was extended southwards from Hartley to Monkseaton and Tynemouth in 1861, and on 27 June 1964 a branch was opened from Monkseaton to Newcastle, crossing over the Newcastle to Berwick line near Benton and then running west of the main line, through Gosforth and Jesmond, to its own terminus at New Bridge Street.

Top left:

The Ponteland branch was included in the Tyneside electrification scheme of the NER, but it was not implemented and operation of the branch became the prerogative at first of BTP 0-4-4T engines on 'autocars', and later of Sentinel steam railcars, until it closed on 17 June 1929. During a tour of the North-East by King George VI and Queen Elizabeth in February 1939 the royal train spent some nights on the branch and was worked by 'V1' 2-6-2Ts Nos 461 and 477. *N. Wilkinson*

Centre left:

Ponteland station buildings in 1960 — 31 years after closure. *K. Hoole*

Below left:

The first electric train left New Bridge Street on 29 March 1904, but the station ceased to exist when Manors North was opened on 1 January 1909. This undated view illustrates the rerailing of an electric car at the end of one of the platforms at New Bridge Street, with the Gateshead steam crane in attendance. The site in the background was being cleared ready for building New Bridge Street goods station. *K. Hoole Collection*

Below:

The Blyth & Tyne Railway was taken over by the North Eastern in 1874 and provided a route from Newcastle to the coast via Backworth, which later became part of the North Tyneside loop. The B&T had its own terminus in Newcastle at New Bridge Street, where ex-B&T 2-4-0 No 1336 was photographed in the 1880s. *LPC*

The junction immediately east of Backworth station in 1960, with the lines to Whitley Bay on the right, and to Earsdon Junction on the left. Although the curve to Earsdon Junction had a third rail this was only for use in the event of an electric train being mistakenly diverted off the electrified lines. Normally the curve was used by the steam trains to Newbiggin. *K. Hoole*

The Blyth & Tyne was taken over by the North Eastern in 1874, and in 1882 the line between Monkseaton and Tynemouth was abandoned in favour of a new route running nearer to the coast, through Whitley Bay and Cullercoats, with a fine new station at Tynemouth. At the same time a connection was put in between the new Tynemouth station and the 1847 Newcastle & North Shields extension to Tynemouth, thus making a loop from Newcastle (Central) to Newcastle (New Bridge Street) via Monkseaton and Backworth. This was the basis of the NER electrification scheme — the final link to complete the circle being the connection between Manors and New Bridge Street opened on 1 January 1909, with Manors North replacing the former Blyth & Tyne terminus.

With the completion of the electrified loop and probably because of long-standing practice, the Morpeth and Newbiggin trains operated from Manors North thus reducing congestion between Manors and Central station. Most of the loop from Heaton through Tynemouth and South Gosforth almost to Jesmond is now used by the Metro trains, although British Rail have a line running parallel with the Metro between the site of Benton East Junction and the site of Back-

worth station to enable BR trains to reach Earsdon Junction and the old Blyth & Tyne line to Hartley, Bedlington and Morpeth.

The Derwent Valley line diverged from the Newcastle to Carlisle route immediately after the latter had crossed the Tyne at Scotswood, and after negotiating the complicated junctions east of Blaydon, arrived at Swalwell at the foot of an almost continuous climb at 1 in 66 over the 10 miles to Blackhill. The stations were Rowlands Gill, Lintz Green (where in 1911 the stationmaster was mysteriously murdered), Ebchester and Shotley

Facing page, top left:
The same location on 24 June 1984. The base of the signalbox remains but the Whitley Bay lines have been taken over by the Metro. The train traversing the curve from Earsdon Junction is a diverted up East Coast express, rerouted via Bedlington because of the Morpeth derailment earlier the same day. The engine is Class 47 No 47595 *Confederation of British Industry*. *Ian S. Carr*

Top right:
Backworth station (which no longer exists) looking west on 22 August 1969; NCB 0-6-0ST No 49 is on the overbridge. *Ian S. Carr*

Centre right:
The site of Backworth station on 24 June 1984, with a diverted Edinburgh-Kings Cross IC125 (from the rear). The Metro tracks are in the foreground. *Ian S. Carr*

Bottom right:
Earsdon Junction, again on 24 June 1984, with an IC125 train diverted because of the Morpeth derailment, this time headed by power car No 43047 *Rotherham Enterprise*. *Ian S. Carr*

Bridge. The line was built under the NER (Conside Branch) Act of 1862 and opened in 1867; beyond Blackhill it connected with the Lanchester Valley branch and a Newcastle-Blackhill-Durham passenger service operated for many years until the Lanchester Valley line closed in 1939. However, by that time the service was down to one train on weekdays and two on Saturdays.

In the 1920s and 1930s some of the trains between Newcastle and Blackhill were worked by steam railcars, including the first Clayton Car No 41 (later No 2121 *Pilot*), and a series of views exist of this car standing in Lintz Green station. The passenger service between Newcastle and Blackhill was withdrawn on 1 February 1954, by which time the only intermediate station still open was Rowlands Gill, but Blackhill station itself did not close until 23 May 1956 as it continued to be served by trains from Newcastle via Birtley, Annfield Plain and Consett.

The Scotswood, Newburn & Wylam line was authorised by an Act of 16 June 1871, which included powers to build a dock at Scotswood. The line, 9¼ miles long, diverged from the Newcastle to Carlisle line at Scotswood and, after passing through Lemington, Newburn, Heddon-on-the-Wall and North Wylam on the north side of the Tyne, rejoined it at West Wylam Junction immediately after crossing the Tyne on an imposing bridge. The line was opened from Scotswood to Newburn in 1875 and on to Wylam in 1876, but the area was one which had known railways for many years; in fact part of the 1876 line ran on the course of the Wylam Wagonway and passed the cottage where George Stephenson was born in 1781. There were other old coal workings in the area, notably at Throckley, and the line served the large steelworks of J. Spencer & Sons Ltd at Newburn, founded in 1822; although the concern became world famous for its products it closed in 1927.

Occasionally passenger trains between Newcastle and Carlisle were routed via Newburn to avoid congestion in the Blaydon area, but the line normally only carried a service between Newcastle and North Wylam, worked in LNER days by steam railcars, and later by a 'G5' 0-4-4T with a push-pull unit. Although the three intermediate stations closed to passengers in 1958 the service to North Wylam continued until 11 March 1968. The line has now been singled and is open only as far as Newburn, 2 miles 58 chains from Scotswood, serving Stella North power station.

Housing development in the Ponteland area northwest of Newcastle led to the NER obtaining a Light Railway Order on 5 November 1900 for a branch from Gosforth to Ponteland; this was opened to goods traffic on 1 March 1905 and to passengers on 1 June 1905. It was tentatively planned to include the branch in the electrification scheme as a means of encouraging traffic, but World War 1 delayed the building of sufficient houses to make electrification viable, and lack of passengers brought about the closure of the branch to passenger traffic on 17 June 1929 although general goods traffic continued until 14 August 1967.

Further housing development was planned at nearby Darras Hall and a branch 1⅛ miles in length was built from Ponteland to Darras Hall under an Act of 20 September 1909; this short branch was opened formally on 27 September 1913, and to the public on 1 October 1913. This line also had a short life — passenger traffic being withdrawn on 17 June 1929; parcels traffic ceased on 5 January 1935 and the end of the line came on 31 July 1954 when freight traffic ceased. The line to Darras Hall was extended privately for 8¾ miles to serve a colliery at Kirkheaton, where a former Glasgow & South Western Railway 0-6-0 survived out of use from 1930 until 1942. The engine was then requisitioned by the Government and, after repairs at Darlington Works,

Top left:
The service between Blyth and Monkseaton via the Avenue branch gave connections into the electric trains to Newcastle. This was worked by a 'G5' on a push-and-pull set, such as No 67261 seen at Monkseaton in September 1957.
Photomatic

Above left:
Dunston, on the outskirts of Gateshead, had a passenger service between 1909 and 1926 worked by a North Eastern 'autocar' — a BTP 0-4-4T engine with a driving coach front and rear, seen here standing on a siding alongside the station. *K. Hoole Collection*

Far left:
The island platform at Dunston remained in place, and with new platform shelters the station was reopened on 1 October 1984 and served by trains from Newcastle to Hexham and Carlisle. *Ian S. Carr*

Left:
Dunston before rehabilitation, photographed on 24 August 1983, with a Newcastle to Hexham DMU passing the weed-grown platform.
Ian S. Carr

Top left:
A diverted Sunday Kings Cross-Edinburgh train passing Dunston on 10 February 1985. *Ian S. Carr*

Top right:
On its way to Carlisle with the empty stock which had formed the 12.15 Blackpool to Newcastle Class 37 No 37026 Loch Awe, with snowploughs, passes Derwenthaugh on 30 June 1984. *Ian S. Carr*

Above:
Before World War 1 the NER operated motor services from Monkseaton station, using Durkopp, Saurer and Fiat charabancs, some with a lightweight roof offering protection for the passengers. *BR*

used at various open-cast and colliery sites in Northumberland until it was finally scrapped in July 1953.

The first train on the Ponteland branch was worked by BTP (Bogie Tank Passenger) 0-4-4T No 1019, but the spread of the NER 'autocar' push-pull units brought No 605 of the same class to the line to work the single coach between South Gosforth and Ponteland. At South Gosforth connection was made with the electric service between New Bridge Street and Central station. The passenger service consisted of 10 trains in each direction daily between South Gosforth and Ponteland, except on Sundays when there were four. On weekdays

This 1914 Maudslay bus carries 'Benton Square' on its indicator, and a service between Benton and Burradon commenced on 2 March 1914. However it was not a success and it was withdrawn on 3 October 1914. Soon afterwards BT 393 was requisitioned by the War Department and the chassis was fitted with a lorry body; the bus body was stored, only to reappear in 1920 on a new Leyland chassis. *BR*

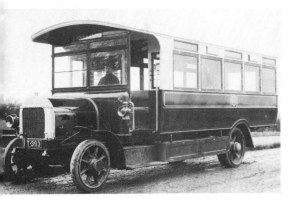

three trains were extended to and from Darras Hall but there was no Sunday service. In the first LNER timetable from 9 July 1923, Darras Hall had the benefit of one extra train in both directions and Ponteland had the luxury of a 10.20pm train from South Gosforth on Saturdays only. The first morning train from Darras Hall (at 7.58am) ran through to Manors North, and the 9.00am from Ponteland ran through to Newcastle Central. In 1929, the year of closure, there were 11 trains between Manors North and Ponteland (12 on Saturdays) of which seven were extended to Darras Hall. Ponteland still had three Sunday trains in each direction.

In 1960 the electrically-controlled set was stabled out of use at Ponteland; this consisted of six ex-NER elliptical-roof compartment coaches, with jumper connections throughout enabling them to be worked by the electric parcels vans. In 1967, following the withdrawal of the North Tyneside electric service, a number of LNER articulated twin units were stored at Callerton awaiting cutting up. The South Gosforth to Ponteland contract was let to W. J. Lant on 30 January 1902 at a figure of £38,661 13s 3d, with R. Blackett being awarded the contract for five stations with stationmaster's houses and cottages at a price of £10,858 10s 0d. The Ponteland to Darras Hall contract, called the 'Little Callerton Railway' by the NER, went to T. Telford Gibb on 15 June 1911 at £2,750. On 19 October 1911 John Craven was given the contract for the

station and a stationmaster's house at Darras Hall at £2,031 5s 8d. At the time the population of Little Callerton numbered 13! To develop the area the owners of the Darras Hall estate presented the land for the railway to the NER and agreed to pay 4% per annum on the assumed cost of £9,000. This £360 was secured by a charge of £2 on each of the 180 five-acre lots into which the estate was divided. When a house was built on any lot it was exonerated from the charge as it was assumed that the occupants would use the railway and the NER would recoup the amount in that way.

Goods traffic was withdrawn from West Gosforth in 1954 but the other stations remained open until the 1960s — Ponteland being the last to close on 14 August 1967. However, the line remains open to Callerton to serve an ICI siding, the final two miles from Kenton Bank Foot to Callerton being over track still owned by BR, but to reach it the BR trains (which also serve Rowntree's siding, between Fawdon and Kenton Bank Foot) have to run over Metro metals from Benton. Where BR trains run 'under the wires' the clearance is raised to a minimum of 4.15m (13ft 7in) instead of the Metro standard of 3.70m (12ft 1in).

The Metro stations are Regent Centre (replacing the NER West Gosforth), Wansbeck Road, Fawdon (replacing Coxlodge) and Kenton Bank Foot (replacing Kenton). A new station named Kingston Park is currently being built between Fawdon and Kenton Bank Foot and will probably be in use by the time this appears in print.

Changes on the west side of Gateshead led to the decision to close the direct goods line from Redheugh to Gateshead up Redheugh incline and to divert the traffic via a new line through Dunston, thus allowing a passenger service to be provided between Dunston-on-Tyne and Newcastle from 1 January 1909. This was operated by a 'steam autocar', commencing with 10 trains in each direction, all calling at Gateshead West. By 1926, when the service succumbed, there were five trains from Newcastle to Dunston and six in the opposite direction with two additional trains in both directions on Wednesday and Saturday evenings; on other days the last train was the 6.22pm from Dunston, and by this time all the trains ran via the King Edward Bridge and thus omitted calling at Gateshead West. With the diversion of Newcastle to Carlisle trains via Dunston from 4 October 1982 it was possible to reopen Dunston station (where the island platform was still in place) and this occurred on 1 October 1984.

6 The North British Gets to Newcastle

Schedule B of the Newcastle & Carlisle and North Eastern Amalgamation Act of 1862 allowed the North British Railway to work its own trains and engines through to Newcastle from Border Counties Junction, west of Hexham, and for many years these were the only 'foreign' engines to be seen regularly on Tyneside. The line was opened throughout to Riccarton Junction on 1 July 1862, and later the same month the Newcastle & Carlisle Railway became part of the NER. Thus the North British trains begin to appear in the NE Working Timetable in 1863, with four trains in both directions, those from Newcastle departing at 6.35am, 12.15pm, 2.40pm and 4.40pm. These stopped at all stations between Newcastle and Hexham except Mickley, and there were two similar trains in both directions on Sundays. The only NB goods arrived at Newcastle at 7.15pm and departed at 11.15pm.

By 1904 the service had been reduced to three passenger trains in both directions; goods trains ran on certain days in the week to Hardengreen (Edinburgh), Portobello, Sighthill (Glasgow) and Riccarton Junction. There was no Sunday passenger service. In 1939 there were still three trains each way, but the 3.50pm waited at Hexham for 28min and allowed passengers to leave Newcastle 30min later by catching the 4.20pm express to Carlisle and changing into the Hawick train at Hexham. The two morning workings were both 'out-and-home' turns for the Blaydon and Hawick engines and men, but on the 3.50pm train the crews exchanged footplates at Reedsmouth, so that the Blaydon men arrived back at Newcastle at 7.54pm and thus a Hawick engine spent Monday, Wednesday and Friday nights at Blaydon shed. The workings were still the same when the service was withdrawn from 15 October 1956. On the final day, Saturday 13 October, the 5.50am from Newcastle was worked by BR Standard Class 3MT 2-6-0 No 77011, the 11.10am by 'K1' 2-6-0 No 62022, and the 4.27pm by 'K3' 2-6-0 No 61968.

An early photograph shows NBR 2-2-2 No 1006 at Prudhoe around the turn of the century, and it was not until the immediate post-World War 1 period (1919/20) that K. A. C. R. Nunn photographed 4-4-2Ts Nos 43 and 48 and 4-4-0 No 213 on the passenger workings: 0-6-0s were seen on goods and passenger workings, including No 191 (later LNER Class J36), No 553 (Class J34), No 667 (Class J36) and No 715 (Class J36).

In the early days of the LNER, 'D31' 4-4-0 No 9312 was stationed at Blaydon to work the Border Counties line from the Newcastle end, and when under repair in February 1927 its place was taken by No 9766 of the same class. At first No 9766 was only on loan from Tweedmouth but this was made permanent early in 1928 and the two former North British engines became a common sight at the west end of Newcastle Central station, until No 9766 was withdrawn in June 1937 and No 9312 in December 1938. Their duties were then taken over by two former North Eastern 'D20' 4-4-0s but these did not prove satisfactory and in January 1939 Class D32 Nos 9887 and 9888 arrived at Blaydon from Tweedmouth for the Border Counties line working; they remained until 1948. As only one engine was required each day a use was found for the other on the 5.53am Newcastle to Darlington (via Bishop Auckland) passenger train, returning via Durham, on the 8.35am Darlington to Newcastle. The engine then carried out various empty stock workings and in the late afternoon and evening worked from Newcastle to Blackhill, returning via Birtley. Finally, it made a return trip to North Wylam before retiring to the shed for the night. On one occasion No 9766 worked a 'Scouts' Jamboree' special from Newcastle to Cockfield Fell, continuing on to Barnard Castle to be turned,

Centre right:
The 4.27pm Newcastle to Riccarton Junction on 16 January 1919 headed by 4-4-2T No 43 and photographed near Scotswood.
LCGB Ken Nunn Collection

Bottom right:
The 10.50am Newcastle to Riccarton Junction arriving at Prudhoe on 15 November 1919, behind 4-4-2T No 48. *LCGB Ken Nunn Collection*

Left:
The North British worked its own trains into Newcastle Central, joining the Carlisle-Newcastle line at Border Counties Junction, west of Hexham, and various types of locomotives were used. This is 0-6-0 No 553 at Prudhoe on 28 June 1920, on the 10.00am from Riccarton Junction.
LCGB Ken Nunn Collection

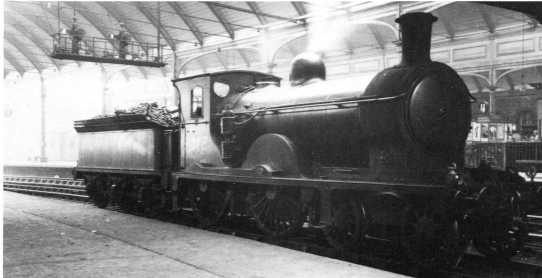

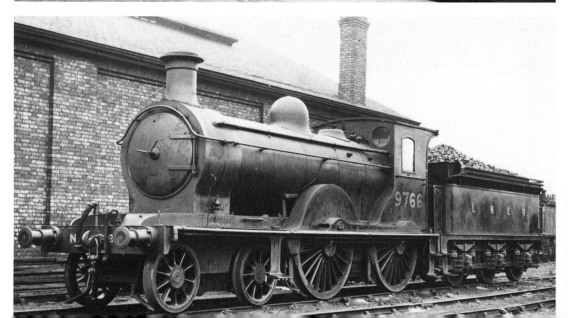

0-6-0 No 715 on a goods train at West Wylam Junction on 3 December 1919.
LCGB Ken Nunn Collection

Centre left:

In LNER days various types of NBR 4-4-0 engines were stationed at Blaydon to work the Border Counties line trains from the Newcastle end, including 'D31' No 9312, photographed in Newcastle Central on 8 August 1936.
W. B. Greenfield

Bottom left:

No 9766, another 'D31', photographed at Blaydon shed. *W. L. Good*

Above:

When the 'D31' engines were withdrawn two ex-NER 'D20' 4-4-0s were used but were not satisfactory and 'D32s' Nos 9887 and 9888 were transferred to Blaydon in January 1939 for the Border Counties duties. This is No 9887 at Blaydon carriage sidings on 31 May 1939.
K. Hoole Collection

before returning with the empty stock to Scotswood Bridge sidings.

In the 1930s former North British engines commenced working into Newcastle from Carlisle after the North British shed at Canal became responsible for the workings formerly performed by the North Eastern shed at London Road. Engines with names painted on their splashers became a common sight — 'D29s' Nos 9360 *Guy Mannering* and 9898 *Sir*

Walter Scott and 'D30s' Nos 9419 *Talisman* (later *The Talisman*) and 9426 *Norna* were a change from the anonymous North Eastern 4-4-0s. These workings continued into the 1950s and visitors in BR livery were 'D30s' Nos 9423 *Quentin Durward*, and 9499 *Wandering Willie*. Occasionally North British Atlantics would arrive, such as 'C11' No 9905 *Buccleuch*.

Workings of North British engines to Newcastle via Berwick were far less common, although Tweedmouth shed became responsible for the NBR engines when that company's shed at Berwick closed. For a period after Grouping, prior to the appearance of the Gresley Pacifics in 1924, North British Atlantics (in NB livery) worked in from Edinburgh on East Coast expresses, and in the 1930s they occasionally appeared at Central station — by then, of course, in LNER green livery; 'C11' No 9878 *Hazeldean* was perhaps the most common.

Wartime transfers took 'J36' 0-6-0s Nos 9172, 9176, 9604, 9622 and 9628 to Borough Gardens shed in the 1940s, and No 9791 spent a short time at Blaydon, but these had all gone by the end of 1943. Five 'J37' 0-6-0s were transferred to Heaton in March 1943 (Nos 9046, 9123, 9274, 9304 and 9435) but they stayed only a few weeks before departing for the Southern Scottish Area. However, the North British connection was maintained until the 1960s by the Haymarket Class A1, A3 and A4 Pacifics — usually in spotless condition — which visited Newcastle daily.

Top:
With the closure of the North Eastern shed at Carlisle London Road the former North British shed at Canal took over the duties and former NBR engines began to appear more frequently on Newcastle trains. Class D30 No 9426 *Norna* was photographed in 1939 at the west end of Central Station. *K. Hoole Collection*

Above:
Another visitor was 'D30' No 9419 *Talisman*, sometimes known as *The Talisman*, also photographed at Central station.
W. B. Greenfield

7 Works and Sheds

Gateshead was the main steam depot on the North Eastern Railway, with daily workings to Edinburgh (124 miles) and Leeds (105½ miles). Following the Grouping the workings were extended to Grantham (163 miles) and later to King's Cross (268 miles). With the Gresley Pacific locomotives the practice was for Gateshead crews to work to Edinburgh and back as a single turn of duty, but the London workings meant lodging in the capital. The most onerous duty was on the prewar non-stop 'Flying Scotsman', where the crews spent three nights away from home, lodging in turn at Edinburgh, London and Edinburgh again, before returning home on the fourth day.

With the headquarters of the Locomotive Department also being at Gateshead (until 1910), the development work on new engines and fittings was usually carried out using Gateshead crews and engines, and the shed, with its important workings, invariably had on its strength the largest and latest NER passenger engines. In the 1870s these were the Fletcher Class 901 2-4-0s, followed by the sole McDonnell design of 4-4-0; then came the various T. W. Worsdell and Wilson Worsdell 4-4-0s and the two, three and four-cylinder Atlantics. For most of their lives the five Raven Pacifics were stationed at Gateshead. In LNER days the Gresley Pacifics were the top link engines, and the solitary water tube boiler engine, No 10000 (for long known as the 'Hush-Hush' because of the secrecy surrounding its construction), was the responsibility of Gateshead shed until 1935. Mention must also

Below:
Gateshead was at one time both the headquarters of the NER Locomotive Department and the main Works, and built and repaired all classes of engines. This view of the interior of the Works was taken in the 1890s and shows Fletcher and Worsdell locomotives.
K. Hoole Collection

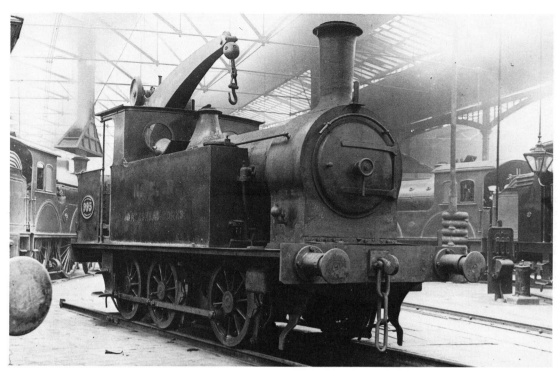

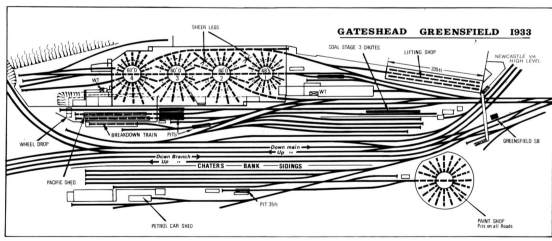

GATESHEAD GREENSFIELD 1933

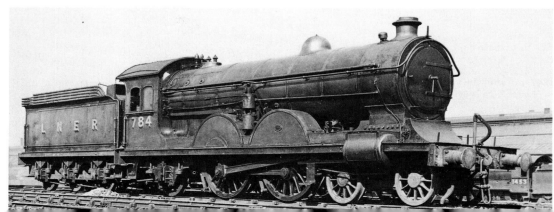

be made of the 'V2' 2-6-2 engines — at one time (1943) there were 42 shedded at Gateshead. The shed was responsible for only some of the local workings around Newcastle, in North Eastern days worked by Class O 0-4-4Ts and Class D 4-4-4Ts; in the 1930s these were replaced by the Gresley 'V1' and 'V3' 2-6-2Ts, which were also used on the Middlesbrough trains. A small stud of Class D49 'Hunt' 4-4-0s was maintained for workings between Newcastle and Carlisle.

Details of the shed itself in its early days are sketchy and although there are frequent references in the NER Minute Books to extensions being authorised it has proved impossible to identify these because the relevant plans have not survived. However it is known that the land for the shed was purchased from a Mr Greene, hence the shed's designation as Greenesfield, although this is more often rendered as Greensfield. For the final years of its existence the shed consisted of a lengthy building containing four turntables in line, serving 74 radiating roads or 'stalls'. Following the closure of the Redheugh branch in 1908 the shed building was extended on its south side so that longer stalls could be constructed to house larger engines, and three electric turntables were provided in 1911/12.

The arrival of the Raven and Gresley Pacifics at Gateshead in the 1920s created problems, both with accommodation and turning; to house these engines (which required a 70ft turntable) the old Gateshead Works tender shop was converted into a three-road straight

shed and became known for obvious reasons as the 'Pacific shed'. Turning difficulties were eased because the layout at the south end of both the High Level Bridge and the King Edward Bridge included a suitable triangle of lines, and it was not until the rebuilding of the shed in the 1950s that a 70ft turntable was provided. There was no space (and probably no money) for a mechanical coaling plant and the shed had to rely on the antiquated NER coaling stage for filling tenders and bunkers.

Space was also severely restricted because of the adjacent locomotive works where at one time the North Eastern's finest and largest locomotives were built. The works grew up in piecemeal fashion, with numerous extensions and changes of use of the various shops. No 1 erecting shop was actually the train shed of the original Gateshead passenger station opened in 1844, when through connections to London were first provided.

George Hudson went all out to create a good impression on Tyneside and the magnificent Gateshead station stood high above the Tyne, looking across to Newcastle, but provided no rail connection across the river. The opening of the High Level Bridge, giving rail access from the south to Newcastle, made Gateshead station redundant and in 1851 it became part of the locomotive works.

Gateshead Works ceased to build new engines in 1910, when this work was transferred to Darlington, but engines continued to be overhauled at Gateshead until 1932. Because of wartime pressure of work at Darlington it was decided to reopen the Works at Gateshead, but closure came for the second time in March 1959. No 1 erecting shop, the former train shed, continued in use for engine repairs by shed staff until the building was demolished in 1968. The hotel serving the 1844 station is still in use, but as offices.

Alterations to the shed in the 1950s brought about the demolition of the building covering two of the turntables, and a few years later the disappearance of steam and the introduction of diesels entailed further changes. These involved converting the remaining building to a straight shed with five roads for the maintenance of diesel locomotives, including the 'Deltics'. The shed was officially closed to steam from 20 March 1965, although steam locomotives remained on its strength until October, when 'B1s' Nos 61019 and 61035 were transferred to York; 'V2' Nos 60868 and 60975 went to St Margarets (Edinburgh) while Nos 60940, 60946 and 60952 were withdrawn. In November 1981 Class 47 diesel No 47402

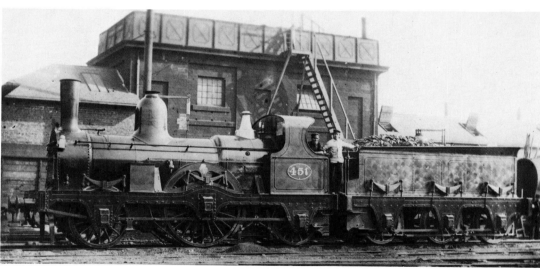

was named *Gateshead* to mark the part the depot had played in supplying engines and men to work East Coast main line trains for more than a century.

Heaton shed was opened on 31 August 1875, originally housing only 13 engines, but it was considerably extended in 1892/93 with the installation of a new 50ft turntable supplied by Messrs Cowans Sheldon of Carlisle. In 1904 this was replaced by a 60ft diameter turntable and the old one was moved to Percy Main. A 70ft turntable suitable for Pacifics was installed at Heaton in 1925. In 1894 plans were to be prepared for a shed to house 132 or 154 engines but the scheme was not implemented, although in 1923 Heaton shed had an allocation of 139 engines. At Grouping the accommodation was provided in an eight-road dead-end building, but in 1930/31 roads 6, 7 and 8 (on the west side) were extended through the south wall to give an exit at that end.

Many of Heaton's workings were to the north on express goods traffic, but pre-1939 the shed had a Pullman working to Leeds, and also express workings to York and Edinburgh. The shed was closed as a major depot in June 1963 and its stud of 50 steam and 14 diesel locomotives dispersed, although the two Quayside electric locomotives, Nos 26500 and 26501, remained at Heaton, on paper at least, until 14 September 1964. Following closure the shed remained in use for storage and repair purposes, and some of Gateshead's 'V2s' were actually condemned whilst standing at Heaton these being Nos 60859, 60940/44/46/52/62.

The locomotive shed at Park Lane Gateshead later known as Borough Gardens, was authorised in 1873, and when it opened two years later it consisted of two circular sheds, each with a 42ft 6in turntable and 20 roads. Two further sheds were added later, again with 20 roads each but with 45ft turntables. One of the larger turntables was later replaced by a 50ft version. The shed's duties were exclusively on freight and shunting work, and in the 1920s and 1930s there was a regular allocation of 25 'Q6' 0-8-0s. For many years the shed also supplied the 'J71' 0-6-0Ts as pilots for Newcastle Central station.

The final allocation consisted of:

K1	2-6-0	1
J25	0-6-0	3
Q6	0-8-0	17
J27	0-6-0	4
J39	0-6-0	8
J71	0-6-0T	2
J72	0-6-0T	8

The shed closed on 13 June 1959 and the buildings were demolished during the following year.

The shed at Blaydon was authorised in 1897 and opened in 1900. Originally it was intended to house 24 engines in a single circular shed with a 50ft turntable, but when an estimated saving of £4,000 a year on light engine workings was considered the shed was doubled in size. Blaydon engines worked mainly on the Carlisle line and on some local services to the west of Newcastle such as the Derwent Valley branch to Blackhill, returning via Lanchester and Durham, or Consett and Birtley.

Blaydon also housed the North British engines used on working the Border Counties line from the Newcastle end; in LNER days these were 'D31' 4-4-0s Nos 9312 and 9766, but when they were withdrawn in 1937/38 two former NER engines were used, namely 'D20s' Nos 2027 and 2028. However, these proved to be unsuitable and 'D32' 4-4-0s Nos 9887 and 9888 were transferred from Tweedmouth to Blaydon for this specific working. North British engines also worked across from Carlisle, more so after the workings from the NER shed at Carlisle (London Road) had been taken over by the former North British shed (Canal), bringing 'D29' and 'D30' 'Scott' 4-4-0s with their evocative names into Newcastle. North British 'C11' Atlantics also appeared occasionally on Carlisle turns, with ex-NB 0-6-0s on freight trains. The final locomotive allocation consisted of 'B1s' Nos 61199 and 61237, 'Q6s' Nos 63362 and 63437, and 'V3' No 67636. The shed was closed on 13 March

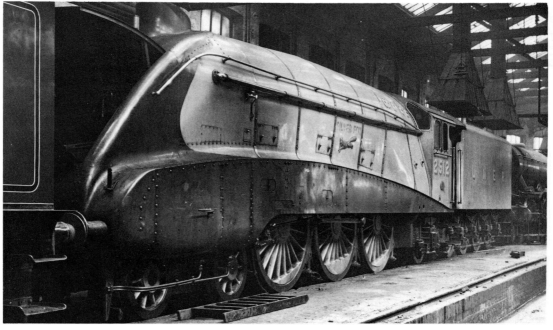

Top:
The LNER fitted new numberplates to all North Eastern engines, including 2-2-4T No 1679. Because of its various rebuildings — on paper it originated as a three-cylinder engine in 1847 — the date was tactfully omitted. *K. Hoole*

Above:
As the turntables in the Gateshead shed were not long enough to take Pacific engines, part of the old tender shop became the 'Pacific Shed', where 'A4' No 2512 *Silver Fox* was photographed in 1935. *W. L. Good*

Above:

The Depot now handles diesel locomotives and an inappropriate visitor on 29 July 1984 was Class 56 No 56133 *Crewe Locomotive Works.*

Ian S. Carr

Below:

Layout of Blaydon Engine Shed as existing in 1934.

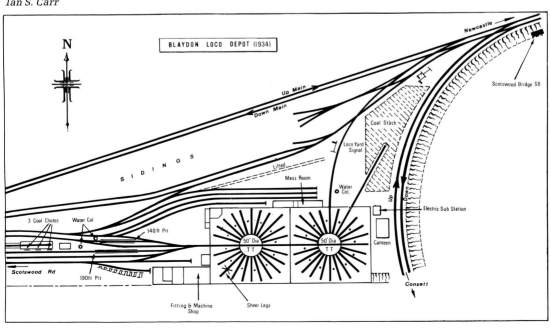

BLAYDON LOCO DEPOT (1934)

N

Newcastle

Scotswood Bridge SB

Up Main

Down Main

Coal Stack

Loco Yard Signal

S I D I N G S

Lifted

Mess Room

Water Col.

Up

Down

Electric Sub Station

3 Coal Chutes

Water Col.

140 ft Pit

Canteen

Scotswood Rd

190ft Pit

50' Dia T T

50' Dia T T

Consett

Fitting & Machine Shop

Sheer Legs

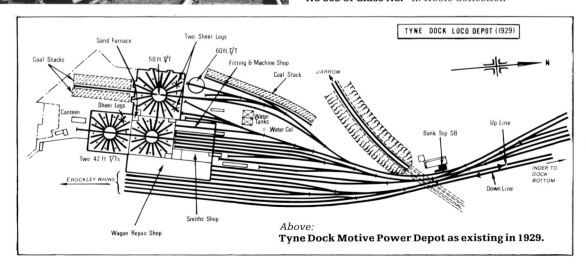

Above:

Tyne Dock Motive Power Depot as existing in 1929.

1965 and demolished during April and May of the following year.

Until demolished in 1966 the buildings at Percy Main retained traces of their Blyth & Tyne Railway parentage. The shed was opened about 1855 and was taken over by the NER in 1874; not only was it the running shed for Blyth & Tyne engines but there were locomotive, carriage and wagon repair shops. The wagon shop appears to have been demolished early in this century when the site was required for the 50ft turntable moved from Heaton in 1904. The locomotive repair shop was badly damaged by fire in January 1921, but was repaired and continued in use until the shed was closed in February 1966. At that time the allocation consisted of 38 diesel shunters; the steam engines — 14 Class J27 0-6-0s — had been transferred away in February 1965.

When Tyne Dock shed opened in 1861/62 it consisted of a straight shed and a circular shed, the latter having a 42ft turntable and 18 radiating roads. A further circular shed, again with a 42ft turntable but this time with 20 roads, was added at the south end about 1870; the final configuration was achieved with the addition of another 20-road circular shed, but with a 50ft turntable, to the west side in 1876.

Engines and crews from Tyne Dock shed worked some of the Newcastle to South Shields and South Shields to Sunderland passenger trains, but the majority of the shed's work was on mineral trains, largely on the former Stanhope & Tyne line down from Consett. It was on this line that the BR Standard Class 9F 2-10-0s became well known because of their excellent work on the vacuum-braked ore trains running between the ore loading plant at Tyne Dock and the Consett Iron Company's

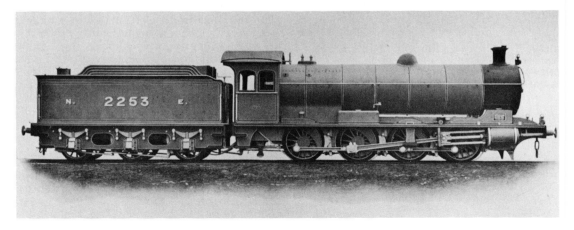

Top left:
Blaydon shed housed both passenger and freight engines, and in this view two 'V1' 2-6-2Ts, two 'Q6's and one 'Q7' are visible. *P. B. Booth*

Centre left:
Percy Main, the old Blyth & Tyne shed, accommodated only 'J27' 0-6-0s in 1954 — 22 of them! This is the actual B&T shed, demolished a few years later, although the depot remained open until 1966, latterly dealing only with diesel shunters. *K. Hoole Collection*

Bottom left:
Following World War 1 Messrs Armstrong Whitworth built 50 'T2' 0-8-0s for the NER; the first engine, No 2253, was formally handed over to Sir Vincent Raven on 12 November 1919, and taken into stock eight days later. It was withdrawn as No 63410 in June 1966.
K. Hoole Collection

Above:
The interior of Armstrong Whitworth's Scotswood Works, with 13 0-6-0s ready for shipment overseas. *K. Hoole Collection*

Below:
An 880hp diesel-electric locomotive built by Armstrong Whitworth in 1933 was tried out on LNER lines radiating from Newcastle.
K. Hoole Collection

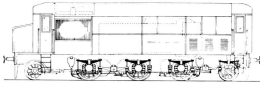

FIG. 16
1-CO-1 4 FT. 8½ IN. GAUGE 800-B.H.P. LOCOMOTIVE BUILT BY
ARMSTRONG WHITWORTH & CO. IN 1933. ARMSTRONG WHITWORTH
4-STROKE ENGINE

works, which are now closed. The shed's final steam allocation consisted of five 'K1' 2-6-0s; Nos 62007/11/45/50 were withdrawn on 9 September 1967 and No 62005, now preserved on the North York Moors Railway, was transferred to Holbeck on the following day. The shed continued to stable a handful of diesel shunters until February 1970.

There were two engine sheds about which little is known. One was at New Bridge Street station and it originated with the extension of the Blyth & Tyne Railway to Newcastle in 1864. This company was taken over by the North Eastern 10 years later and, although the main shed was at Percy Main, some engines were stationed in the two-road shed at New Bridge Street, which was situated on the northwest side of the passenger station adjacent to Ellison Terrace.

In October 1901 it was reported to the NER Locomotive & Stores Committee that the shed would have to be demolished to make way for the connecting line between the former Blyth & Tyne terminus and the NER line at Manors, and that a replacement shed would be required. It was decided to build the new shed at South Gosforth and a tender of £480 was accepted for a two-road shed 150ft long and 31ft wide. The result was a corrugated iron coated structure, with a large ventilator along the top of the curved roof. The probable date of opening was 19 December 1902 but it seems to have had a very short life as there are indications, but no actual proof, that it closed on 1 August 1904. The site of the shed was in the triangle of lines formed by the two connections to the Ponteland branch from the South Gosforth to Benton line. A water column remained in place for many years afterwards.

8 Signalboxes

The history of the signalboxes in the New-castle and Gateshead area is extremely complicated and at least three boxes, Nos 1, 2 and 3 existed at Central station in 1875. The earliest photograph it has been possible to locate is in the National Railway Museum collection and shows a box built in the centre of a gantry spanning five tracks at the east end of the station, with five posts having two semaphore signals each, one for each direction, and two posts each with a single signal controlling the entrance to the station. The box was reached by means of the spiral stairway in the supporting girders on the north side.

In the alterations to the station carried out between 1893 and 1895, a long brick-built box with 244 levers was erected on the north side of the station, at the east end, adjacent to the parcels platform and the new bay platforms. This survived until the opening of a gantry box, also known as Newcastle No 1, which spanned the tracks leading to the three through platforms. This box, opened in 1909, was operated electro-pneumatically and lasted until 1959 when it was replaced by an electric box built over Platform 10 and the carriage sidings on the south side of the station.

No 2 box was at the centre of the station, at the inner ends of Platforms 6 and 7, and it controlled the movements in the station itself. It was altered to electro-pneumatic operation in 1906, in connection with the opening of the King Edward VII bridge, and had 67 levers. No 3 box was another brick structure on the south side of the Carlisle lines at the west end of the station; it was replaced in 1906 with a new box in the 'V' of the junction between the Carlisle lines and those over the King Edward

Below:
The NER was noted for the multiplicity of its semaphore signals. This is the west end of Newcastle Central before the building of the King Edward Bridge. *K. Hoole Collection*

Top:
The gantry at the west end in 1950, operated from No 3 signalbox. *BR*

Above:
The change in appearance after the replacement of the semaphores in 1959. *K. Hoole Collection*

Top:
Newcastle No 1 signalbox was a bridge cabin dating from 1909 and the installation of the electro-pneumatic system. It was replaced in 1959. *C. Myton*

Below:
The interior of No 2 box situated inside the station and responsible for controlling platforms 8 and 9 and the two sidings in between. It was replaced in 1959 and the box itself was destroyed in a spectacular fire in 1961. *W. B. Greenfield*

Top:
The interior of No 3 box in the 'V' of the junction between the Carlisle lines and those over King Edward Bridge. *W. B. Greenfield*

Below:
King Edward Bridge signalbox at the south end of the King Edward Bridge. The up East Coast train is approaching on the eastern-most tracks across the bridge (usually used by freight trains and light engines) but it is about to cross on to the main lines to the south. *K. Hoole*

Top:
The diagram in King Edward Bridge signalbox.
W. B. Greenfield

Above:
The interior of Manors bridge cabin, destroyed by fire in 1943. *W. B. Greenfield*

Facing page, top left:
The diagram in the replacement Manors signalbox on the platform at Manors station.
C. Myton

Top right:
Changing styles (1): Tynemouth North signalbox. *C. Myton*

Bottom right:
Pontop Crossing was another electro-pneumatic signalbox, but when it had a manual frame fitted the box had to be doubled in size, as the brickwork of the building indicates. *K. Hoole*

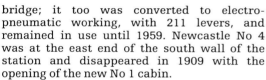

bridge; it too was converted to electro-pneumatic working, with 211 levers, and remained in use until 1959. Newcastle No 4 was at the east end of the south wall of the station and disappeared in 1909 with the opening of the new No 1 cabin.

In 1887 there is mention of an 'octagon cabin' at Castle Junction, (the junction between the lines off the High Level Bridge and those entering Central station from the north); for some reason this was provided in connection with the widening of the Manors to Heaton section to four tracks; the widening between Castle Junction and Manors did not take place until the additions and alterations of 1893-95. The 1892 Appendix to the Working Timetable lists a box called High Level Bridge and in contemporary photographs this is shown as having been situated at the north end of the bridge on the east side of the lines; a similar box, Dean Street, was perched on the south side of the tracks to Manors just east of the Castle Keep and this also appears in pre-1909 photographs. The approach by signalmen going on duty was along a narrow

footway with railings on both sides, along the top of the boundary wall.

Another gantry box spanned the four tracks at the west end of Manors station, and controlled the junction between the north main lines and the 1909 connection to the Blyth & Tyne route through Jesmond; also under its jurisdiction were the cross-overs used for routing trains into Central. It must be remembered that from Heaton South Junction to Manors the up and down main lines and up and down Tynemouth lines ran parallel, with the electric services on the south-east side and the main line trains on the north-west side; however, the platforms at Central were not suitable for this arrangement and trains on the two routes had exchange positions so that the electrics could run into the bay platforms on the north side of the station and the main line trains into the through platforms on the south side. In addition there were the trains via Jesmond but normally they left and joined the Manors to Central section on the correct side of the line and used the two northern tracks. Goods and mineral trains from the Manors

Top:
**Changing styles (2): Tynemouth South
signalbox.** *C. Myton*

Below:
**The bridge cabins were susceptible to fires,
usually caused by sparks from a locomotive
setting fire to the birds' nests below the cabin.
Pelaw suffered this fate in 1956 and 1958 and as a
result it was decided to build a normal cabin,
which was completed in 1960.** *C. Myton*

Top right:
**The unusual signalbox at Forest Hall, with the
Newcastle & Berwick Railway buildings in the
background.** *Lens of Sutton*

Bottom right:
**The Newcastle panel signalbox brought into use
in 1959 was constructed across Platform 10 and
the adjacent carriage sidings on the south side of
Central station. In this January 1957 view,
building work is well advanced and the intended
outline of the structure already evident.** *BR*

FOREST HALL STATION

Top:
The control room of the then new Newcastle panel signalbox in 1959. Like the pioneering scheme at York completed in 1951, the system was of the 'one control switch' (OCS) type, whereby the turning of a thumb switch set all the points and signals for a given section of route. *BR*

Above:
Benton panel took over the functions of the old Benton Quarry box, together with those of Benton East and Backworth boxes, on 1 March 1964. It was later abolished with the introduction of Tyne & Wear Metro services. *BR*

direction approached Central on the up Tynemouth line so that they could be held to await a path over the crossings at the north end of the High Level Bridge, and then run outside the station to join the King Edward Bridge or Carlisle routes. Consequently there was a lot of juggling to avoid conflicting movements and delay, and close co-operation between the No 1 and Manors signalmen was necessary.

The gantry box at Manors was converted to partial electric operation in June 1936, with colour light signals installed on the various lines, but it was destroyed by fire on 13 June 1943. A temporary box was provided but it was not until January 1945 that a new box was opened at the south end of Manors station, actually on the station platform. It was closed in 1959 with the opening of the Newcastle electric box. Two-way working on the main lines between Manors and Newcastle No 1 was brought into use on 13 December 1937. Heaton Station, Argyle Street, Ouseburn and Riverside boxes closed on 2 February 1964 when control of all points and signals was transferred to the Newcastle panel box, and a week later the second stage brought about the demise of Manors North, Jesmond and West Jesmond boxes. A new electric box named Heaton

opened on 6 September 1964, replacing Heaton South Junction and Benton Bank. The next box to the north, Benton Quarry, was closed on 1 March 1964, when its duties were taken over by a new box at Benton, which also took control of Benton East and Backworth, but it became redundant with the introduction of the Metro.

An early gantry box spanned the three tracks at the south end of the High Level Bridge, just off the platform ends of Gateshead East and Gateshead West stations, but this disappeared in the 1890s; in the 1870s it was known as Team Valley Junction but it later became High Level Bridge, and the replacement was known as Gateshead Junction. This final box was closed in 1929 and the junction was then worked from Greensfield box at the opposite end of Gateshead West station, which also controlled the outlet from the locomotive depot, making it one of the busiest boxes in the North-East. At the opposite end of Gateshead East station was High Street box where an accident to an electric train from South Shields took place on 13 January 1954. Due to wear on the electro-pneumatic equipment there was a malfunction of the facing points and the leading bogie of the first coach of the electric train took the correct route into Gateshead

Above and top:

The new panel signalbox at Gateshead (top) which commenced operation in December 1962, inherited a control area previously in the charge of five old installations. It contained a control system of the 'Entrance/Exit' (NX) type, so-called because the operation of two buttons on the route-indicating panel (above) at the entrance and exit points of the selected path set the relevant points and signals as required. This system, with improvements since made possible by subsequent advances in technology, has become the standard equipment for the major area resignalling schemes of today. *BR*

Left:
Exterior (above) and interior (left) of the new box opened at Pelaw on 2 October 1960. *BR*

East station, whereas the rear bogie of the same coach took the route to Greensfield, on the other side of the signal box. In colliding almost broadside on with the box the leading coach No E29191E was severely damaged and it was withdrawn in May 1954. This was actually a replacement car built in 1928 (as LNER No 23253) to replace a previous No 23253 damaged beyond repair in the collison at Manors on 7 August 1926. This in

turn had replaced the original No 3253 destroyed in the Heaton Car Sheds fire in 1918.

The various Gateshead boxes — King Edward Bridge, Greensfield, High Street, Park Lane and Borough Gardens — were closed on 9 December 1962 with the opening of the Gateshead electric box; the first four of the old boxes were Westinghouse electro-pneumatic installations dating back to 1905/6, and Westinghouse Brake & Signal Co Ltd carried out much of the internal work in the new box. This box linked up with the electric box at Pelaw opened on 2 October 1960, which replaced the Pelaw gantry box, and boxes at Felling, Wardley, Hebburn West and Boldon Colliery. On the Team Valley line, Tyne box took over the function previously carried out by Low Fell, Low Fell Sidings, Lamesley, Birtley North, Birtley Station, Ouston, Chester-le-Street, Chester Moor, Plawsworth and Kimblesworth over the last two week-ends in April 1963.

9 Goods and Mineral Traffic

Central Newcastle was served by two large goods stations, namely those at Trafalgar (replaced in 1907 by New Bridge Street) and Forth. Trafalgar goods station was opened in 1850 and, according to W. W. Tomlinson, it was there that the first application of hydraulic power for railway purposes was made on cranes that gave many years of trouble free service. As a result of the construction of the New Bridge Street to Manors connection, Trafalgar goods was closed on 2 January 1907 in readiness for its demolition. To replace it a fine new building was erected on the other (north) side of New Bridge Street itself and this took the name of the thoroughfare on to which it faced; it was situated in the southeast corner of the former Blyth & Tyne yard but necessitated the purchase of additional land, and the demolition of properties on the west side of Falconer Street, Shieldfield Green and Pleasant Row.

This new goods station was built in ferro-concrete using the Hennebique method and it covered an area 180ft by 430ft; it was

Below:

Coal was once the lifeblood of Newcastle and the Tyne, but now it has lost much of its importance. Until the replacement of the low level stone bridge by the present swing bridge in 1876, only very small vessels could proceed further upstream. The removal of this obstacle and constant dredging allowed colliers to reach the coal staiths, and naval vessels to reach the fitting-out berths in the Dunston and Elswick areas respectively. Dunston is on the south (Gateshead) bank of the river, and Elswick on the north. The NER opened Dunston staiths in 1893. This is Dunston in 1947, with ships tied up in the river after World War 2. *BR*

92ft high, with the rail traffic handled in the basement and on the first floor, with the two upper floors used for the storage of goods. This striking building suffered severe damage from German bombing on 28 September 1941. The warehouse was full of items such as sugar, grain, linseed, cattle feed etc, and the wooden grain chutes between floors allowed the fire to spread rapidly among the contents and, in fact, the place burned for weeks. Even so it was still possible to use parts of the building, largely due to the method of construction used, until it was closed on 4 December 1967 and subsequently demolished.

Forth goods station, west of Central station, opened in 1871. The building was originally 460ft long and 340ft wide; it was extended at the western end in 1892/93, increasing the length to 609ft. Approximately 1,400 staff were employed in 1900 and this figure included 95 shunters and 176 rulleymen, with 185 horses for drawing the rulleys on the daily deliveries; 1,100,000 tons of miscellaneous traffic and 800,000 head of livestock were handled annually. Specimen figures for 1913 included 36,559 tons of flour and bran, and 10,517 tons of ale and ale empties, together with 16,832 wagons of livestock.

Because of its position on the river bank it was possible to build the northern approach to the King Edward Bridge through the roof of the Forth goods warehouse, by simply cutting a

Above left:
Dunston staiths were extended in 1898 and by 1911 were handling 3,523,000 tons of coal a year. This view was taken in 1958, with loading completed in the SS *Charles Parsons* of the CEGB. *BR*

Far left:
Much of the coal shipped at Dunston was bound for the London power stations but the Stella North power station, on the former Scotswood Newburn & Wylam line, receives its coal direct from collieries in County Durham, as on this working with Class 56 No 56076 *Blyth Power*, **photographed on 28 October 1983.** *Ian S. Carr*

Above:
The same engine, No 56076, returning with the empties and passing the site of Scotswood station. The line on the left to Blaydon has now been abandoned following the re-routeing of the Carlisle trains through Dunston. *Ian S. Carr*

Below:
Howdon-on-Tyne station with Class 37s Nos 37001 and 37068 heading an air-braked coal train bound for Blyth power station on 19 June 1979. *Ian S. Carr*

Top:
The approach to Newcastle Central station over the King Edward Bridge, illustrating how the line was cut through Forth Goods station. *K. Hoole*

Above:
A down coal train takes the slow line at Ouston Junction, behind Class 20s Nos 20193 and 20159 on 24 March 1979. The Tyne Dock to South Pelaw line, once used by the '9F'-hauled ore trains to Consett, ran on the embankment and overbridge in the background. *Ian S. Carr*

Top right:
An old established working was that from Boldon Colliery, over BR metals, to reach the former Harton Coal company's lines at South

Shields. On 14 August 1962 two NCB 0-6-0ST engines and their brake vans were photographed approaching Pontop Crossing. *Ian S. Carr*

Centre right:
Clayton Bo-Bo diesel-electric No 8597 heading west towards Pelaw clatters over Pontop Crossing on 25 June 1970. On the right are the remains of Pontop Crossing signalbox, destroyed five days earlier by a fire started by vandals. *Ian S. Carr*

Right:
Pontop Crossing in happier days as '9F' 2-10-0 No 92097 heads for Consett on an ore train on 3 May 1966. *B. Webb*

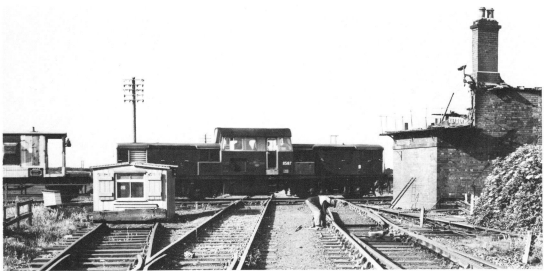

Top left:
The closure of the Stanhope & Tyne route from Green Lane (South Shields) to South Pelaw sent the ore trains round via Pelaw and Gateshead. Here Class 24s Nos D5103 and D5102 approach Pelaw on 21 July 1969. *Ian S. Carr*

Bottom left:
Tyne Yard was built in the Team Valley to handle the freight traffic for the area; this view, taken in 1963, was looking north towards Gateshead, with the Control Tower on the right. *BR*

Above:
Class 37s Nos 37029 and 37165 arrive at Tyne Yard with Workington to Lackenby steel empties on 28 October 1983. *Ian S. Carr*

Below:
Class 03 shunter No 03066 entering Tyne Yard with five wagons of scrap metal from Dunston on 24 June 1984. *Ian S. Carr*

slice the width of four tracks out of the roof. The cut ends were then glazed, and from trains passing over the bridge it was possible to look through broken panes down to the floor of the warehouse. Forth Goods was closed and subsequently demolished, but a few sidings remained in use until 1983.

On 15 October 1963, Dr Beeching formally opened Tyneside's new Central Freight Depot, built at Gateshead on the site of the former Borough Gardens Motive Power Depot and adjacent sidings. This took two years to build and cost 'just over a million pounds' according to a press release issued at the time. It was intended to serve an area of 700sq miles, replacing goods stations between Blyth and Chester-le-Street and between Consett and South Shields.

A few months earlier, on 28 June 1963, the new Tyne Marshalling Yard was opened by Lord Hailsham. This had been built on a

Top:
A ballast train leaves the north end of Tyne Yard on 26 April 1984 with Class 40 No 40150 in charge. *Ian S. Carr*

Above:
Numerous colliery companies in Durham and Northumberland purchased redundant locomotives from the main line railways to handle their coal and passenger traffic. The South Shields, Marsden & Whitburn Colliery branch of the Harton Coal Co operated a passenger service intended for the miners living in South Shields and working at Whitburn Colliery, but the trains were available to the public. The station at South Shields was at Westoe Lane and HCC No 4 (ex-NER No 1333 of Class 398) is awaiting departure for Whitburn in 1946. The double-window cab is a colliery company's addition as no Class 398 engines had them when on the NER or LNER. *L. W. Perkins*

135-acre site located four miles south of Newcastle, on the west side of the East Coast main line, adjacent to the Team Valley Trading Estate. Ten coal seams lie under the yard and, if the coal had been extracted, a subsidence of 7ft could have been expected, so that BR had to reserve the coal under the whole of the yard. As the site was low-lying 2,250,000cu yd of filling had to be used, partly from local colliery tips, but also some 300,00cu yd from near Corbridge, on the Newcastle to Carlisle line, where a new cutting was made to replace a tunnel in need of heavy repairs. A further 360,000cu yd came from a new cutting north of Durham where it was planned to realign the main line.

The Control Tower at the south end of the yard houses two separate installations, one controlling the traffic in the yard itself, and the other controlling trains on the main line. As built the yard contained 104 sidings comprising 54 miles of track, 75% of which had been recovered from redundant lines and sidings.

Facing page, bottom:
The Pelaw Main company used ex-NER Class H 0-4-0Ts for shunting, some of which were usually to be found at the shed at Wrekenton on the southern outskirts of Gateshead where No 1310 was photographed. *K. Hoole Collection*

Above:
The Seaton Delaval Colliery stock included a Great Northern 0-6-0 purchased from the Darlington dealer J. F. Wake, and this was photographed after overhaul by Wake and awaiting despatch to its new owners. *K. Hoole Collection*

Below:
The Bowes Railway used steam locomotives at its eastern and western ends, with rope-worked inclines separating the two sections. One of the engines used between Springwell Bank Foot and the staiths at Jarrow was ex-GWR No 713, originally Barry Railway No 52, photographed in its GWR livery soon after arriving from Swindon in 1936. *K. Hoole Collection*

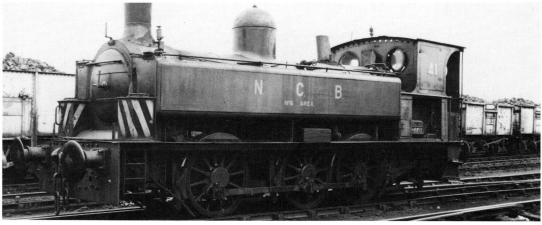

Top:
One of the most unusual colliery locomotives in the North East was Cramlington Coal Co's No 15, an outside-cylinder 2-6-0 built by Beyer Peacock in 1895 for an overseas railway but purchased by the Midland & South Western Junction Railway. It was M&SWJR No 14, and J. F. Wake bought the frames, cylinders and wheels, fitted a boiler and cab and then sold it to the Cramlington company. It lasted in Northumberland until 1943. *R. H. Inness/K. Hoole Collection*

Above:
The Consett Iron Co used a short-wheelbase

0-6-0PT and, although it was not purchased from the NER, the North Eastern had a similar engine, namely No 994, obtained from Kitson & Co in 1875 and sold to John Bowes & Partners in 1891. Some of the Consett engines passed to the National Coal Board and this engine, Consett Iron Co No A5, NCB No 41, is now preserved. This view was taken at Derwenthaugh on 18 July 1968. *B. Webb*

Below:
A 1,000-ton coal train approaching Newcastle on a test run from Morpeth behind the pioneer Class X 4-8-0T No 1350. *K. Hoole Collection*

10 The Tyne & Wear Metro

The new County of Tyne & Wear is the major industrial and commercial centre in northeast England with a population of 1.2 million, mostly based on Tyneside and Wearside. The Tyneside area is divided by the River Tyne, with Newcastle-upon-Tyne on the north bank and Gateshead on the south. Relying for many years on heavy industries such as coal and shipbuilding, the shape of the transport system remained comparatively static during the first 60 years of the 20th century, with trams (later buses) serving the inner areas, and the North Eastern electric trains (introduced in 1904) serving the coastal area north of the Tyne and from 1938 the Pelaw, Jarrow and South Shields branch.

Below:
Three bridges now cross the Ouseburn valley — Ouseburn Viaduct (rail), Byker Bridge (road) and Byker Viaduct (Metro) — and all are visible in this picture. The road bridge is on the left and the rail bridge on the right; in the centre the overhead catenary is being erected on the Metro bridge on 4 August 1981. *Ian S. Carr*

Proximity to the river was not an essential requirement for the new light industries, and they could be located over a large area around Newcastle and Gateshead; when considered in conjunction with the spread of housing development into the more salubrious areas this factor leant urgency to the need for the establishment of an improved transport system, preferably integrating road and rail services.

The decision not to concentrate solely on buses but to use them to feed passengers on to a rail system led to the Metro plan. This was made possible by the 1968 Transport Act, whereby Government grants could be made towards approved public transport investments on the same basis as for road investment; this enabled Passenger Transport Authorities and Executives to be set up with specific responsibility for the planning, integration and operation of public transport in their areas.

The Tyneside Passenger Transport Authority and Executive were created in 1969, with the Authority responsibility for policy and

Above:
A Metro train on Byker Viaduct; again all three bridges are visible. *Tyne & Wear PTE*

Above right:
The control centre of the Metro system is at South Gosforth station, where a new building on the down platform houses various offices, train and power control rooms and staff facilities. Immediately north of the station the tracks diverge; to the left to Bank Foot (originally the NER Ponteland branch), and to the right to Backworth and on to Tynemouth (the Blyth & Tyne line of 1864). South Gosforth retains its NER footbridge. The photograph was taken on 8 April 1980, with a Metro train on a crew training trip. *Ian S. Carr*

Bottom right:
Interior view of the South Gosforth Metro Control Centre. *Tyne & Wear PTE*

finance, and the professional Executive for the planning and integration of local public transport. After undertaking lengthy studies of the transport needs of Tyneside, application was made to Parliament for the necessary powers and the Tyneside Metropolitan Railway Act received the Royal Assent in July 1973; construction of the Metro system commenced in the following year.

Basically the plan was to take over the British Rail lines and stations north of the Tyne from near Heaton through Tynemouth, Whitley Bay, Benton and South Gosforth to Jesmond (where the line would go underground) and also part of the Ponteland branch from South Gosforth to Bank Foot. South of the Tyne the network would run from Gateshead to South Shields, with a diversion approaching South Shields to serve a more populous area. The two sections were to be connected by an underground link under Newcastle and Gateshead, and a new bridge across the Tyne. New and refurbished stations were to total 41, later amended to 42 (and further stations are already being built), with a total route mileage of 34 miles.

Due to various reasons the first section from Haymarket to Tynemouth was not opened until August 1980, followed by the branch from South Gosforth to Bank Foot in May 1981. The cross-river link to Heworth was opened in

Top:
South Gosforth station in the 1960s, before the advent of the Metro. *A. J. Wickens*

Above:
Percy Main station in BR days. *K. Hoole Collection*

Above:
Percy Main as modernised for the Metro.
Tyne & Wear PTE

Below:
The northwestern terminus at Bank Foot with the standard Metro nameboard and shelter.
Tyne & Wear PTE

Above:
 A Bank Foot to Heworth Metro train passes BR Class 31 No 31324 with Speedlink vans from Rowntree's factory near Fawdon on 24 August 1983. The BR trains share the same tracks as far as Benton, where BR territory is reached via the southwest curve. *Ian S. Carr*

Below:
At the opposite end of the Metro system, at Pelaw, a BR tamping machine takes the Leamside line as a Metro train from Bank Foot continues (empty) from Heworth to South Shields on 4 March 1984.
Ian S. Carr

Above:
BR Class 56 No 56112 takes the Jarrow line at Pelaw with an oil tank train from Teesport. The Sunderland line is in the foreground, with a South Shields Metro train crossing on 9 May 1984. *Ian S. Carr*

Below:
A South Shields to Bank Foot Metro train leaves the new station at Bede on 24 March 1984, the first day of public service between South Shields and Heworth. *Ian S. Carr*

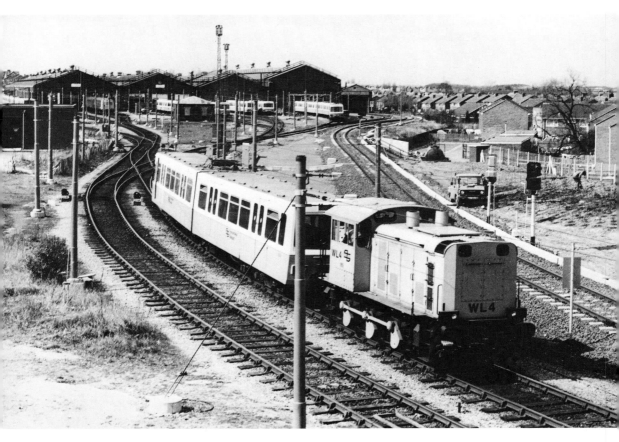

Above:
The changed scene at South Gosforth car sheds after being taken over by the Metro from British Rail. Works Locomotive No 4 is shunting a Metro unit. *Ian S. Carr*

November 1981, and the North Tyne network was completed in November 1982 with the opening of the St James to Tynemouth section. The extension from Heworth to South Shields was opened in March 1984, completing the system, although its success has led to a demand for extensions, particularly to Newcastle Airport.

The first Metro cars were exhibited at the Stockton & Darlington Railway 150th Anniversary celebrations at Shildon in 1975 and thus there was a five-year period in which to overcome any technical obstacles, and to develop the best form of track, overhead construction, and station buildings on the test track established near Backworth. Most interesting are those sections inherited from the North Eastern Railway, and although great changes have taken place it is still possible to recognise certain NER features. However Tynemouth station, now more than a century old, is no advertisement for the Metro but this is no fault of the PTE and is due to difficulties regarding its demolition and replacement by a modern station better suited to the needs of the 1980s.

A drawback of the North Eastern electric lines was that, although convenient for anyone arriving at Newcastle by train, they were convenient neither for the shopping centre nor for tram and bus connections to outlying areas. Now there is access to the Metro from the concourse at Central station giving a frequent service to all points on the system and, in the opposite direction, making it easier for anyone living in the suburbs to join the main line trains at Central station. However, in spite of the fact that large areas south and west of Gateshead and Newcastle derive no benefit from the network the inhabitants of the Tyneside conurbation appear to appreciate the Metro and the integrated bus services which complement it.

11 Locomotive Allocations

Gateshead Locomotive Allocation
6 December 1923

LNER Class	NER Class		
A2	4-6-2	4-6-2	2400, 2401
B14	S1	4-6-0	2111, 2112, 2113, 2114, 2115
B16	S3	4-6-0	920, 2363, 2365, 2367, 2369, 2371, 2375, 2377, 2379, 2381
C6	V	4-4-2	295, 1753, 1794
C6	V/09	4-4-2	696, 701, 704, 705
C7	Z	4-4-2	706, 709, 716, 718, 719, 720, 722, 727, 728, 729, 732, 733, 734, 735, 736, 737, 2170, 2204, 2205, 2206, 2209, 2212
C8	4CC	4-4-2	730, 731
D17/1	M	4-4-0	1621, 1625, 1631, 1634, 1636, 1638
D17/2	Q	4-4-0	1880, 1909, 1927
D20	R	4-4-0	1051, 1147, 1184, 1206, 1209, 1223, 1235, 1236, 1258, 1665, 2016, 2030, 2105, 2107
D22	F	4-4-0	1546
F8	A	2-4-2T	423, 804
G5	O	0-4-4T	1788, 1916, 1920, 2093, 2095, 2100
G6	BTP	0-4-4T	955
H1	D	4-4-4T	1517, 2153, 2154, 2155, 2156
J21	C	0-6-0	51, 107, 259, 313, 1614, 1811, 1817, 1819
J25	P1	0-6-0	1714, 2062
J71	E	0-6-0T	221, 338, 811, 1688
J72	E1	0-6-0T	1722, 1728, 1741, 2177, 2316
J77	290	0-6-0T	324
J78	H1	0-6-0T	995
J79	H2	0-6-0T	1662
N8	B	0-6-2T	1127
N10	U	0-6-2T	1321, 1716
Y7	H	0-4-0T	1304, 1307, 1800

Total 114

Gateshead Locomotive Allocation
1 January 1939

A1	4-6-2	2571 Sunstar, 2572 St Gatien, 2574 St Frusquin, 2575 Galopin, 2576 The White Knight
A3	4-6-2	2501 Colombo, 2503 Firdaussi, 2505 Cameronian, 2507 Singapore, 2573 Harvester, 2595 Trigo, 2596 Spearmint, 2597 Gainsborough, 2598 Blenheim, 2599 Book Law, 2746 Fairway
A4	4-6-2	2511 Silver King, 4462 Great Snipe, 4463 Sparrow Hawk, 4465 Guillemot, 4469 Gadwall, 4499 Pochard, 4500 Garganey, 4901 Capercaillie
A8	4-6-2T	2146, 2154, 2161
C6	4-4-2	699, 704
C7	4-4-2	716, 721, 733, 734, 735, 736, 2167, 2201, 2212
C9	4-4-2	727, 2171
D49	4-4-0	201 The Bramham Moor, 211 The York and Ainsty, 232 The Badsworth, 273 The Holderness, 361 The Garth, 362 The Goathland, 363 The Grafton, 364 The Grove
G5	0-4-4T	526, 1838
J21	0-6-0	313, 1614, 1817, 1819
J71	0-6-0T	103, 179, 221, 248, 501, 1690
J72	0-6-0T	1720, 1722, 1741, 2177, 2313, 2335
K3	2-6-0	1100, 1101, 1102, 1108, 1302, 1304, 1318, 2458, 2465, 3825, 3826
N10	0-6-2T	1321, 1716
Q5	0-8-0	578, 645
V1	2-6-2T	415, 416, 454, 455, 466
Y1	0-4-0T	79, 150, 175, 183
Y3	0-4-0T	197

Total 91

Gateshead Locomotive Allocation
1 October 1954

A1	4-6-2	60115 *Meg Merrilies*, 60124 *Kenilworth*, 60129 *Guy Mannering*, 60132 *Marmion*, 60135 *Madge Wildfire*, 60137 *Redgauntlet*, 60142 *Edward Fletcher*, 60143 *Sir Walter Scott*, 60145 *Saint Mungo*, 60147 *North Eastern*, 60150 *Willbrook*, 60151 *Midlothian*, 60154 *Bon Accord*, 60155 *Borderer*
A2	4-6-2	60516 *Hycilla*, 60518 *Tehran*, 60521 *Watling Street*, 60538 *Velocity*
A3	4-6-2	60038 *Firdaussi*, 60040 *Cameronian*, 60042 *Singapore*, 60060 *The Tetrarch*, 60070 *Gladiateur*, 60075 *St Frusquin*, 60076 *Galopin*, 60078 *Night Hawk*, 60082 *Neil Gow*
A4	4-6-2	60001 *Sir Ronald Matthews*, 60002 *Sir Murrough Wilson*, 60005 *Sir Charles Newton*, 60016 *Silver King*, 60018 *Sparrow Hawk*, 60019 *Bittern*, 60020 *Guillemot*, 60023 *Golden Eagle*
B1	4-6-0	61011 *Waterbuck*, 61012 *Puku*, 61013 *Kopi*, 61019 *Nilghai*, 61022 *Sassaby*, 61100, 61199, 61238 *Leslie Runciman*
D20	4-4-0	62360, 62375, 62396
G5	0-4-4T	67259
J39	0-6-0	64701, 64704, 64852, 64865, 64869, 64871, 64929
J71	0-6-0T	68270, 68272, 68283, 68309, 68314
J72	0-6-0T	68674, 68675, 68680, 68693, 68720, 68723, 68732, 68744, 69005
N10	0-6-2T	69090, 69091, 69092, 69095, 69109
V2	2-6-2	60802, 60807, 60809 *The Snapper, The East Yorkshire Regiment, The Duke of York's Own*, 60868, 60883, 60923, 60940, 60947, 60949, 60957, 60964, 60967
V3	2-6-2T	67634, 67682, 67683, 67687, 67688, 67689, 67690
Y1	0-4-0T	68159, 68160

Total 94

Gateshead Locomotive Allocation
1 January 1971

03	2048, 2050, 2052, 2053, 2055, 2056, 2058, 2059, 2060, 2064, 2066, 2071, 2074, 2078, 2094, 2103, 2104, 2105, 2106, 2108, 2110, 2147, 2156, 2163, 2165, 2170
08	3072, 3073, 3195, 3243, 3244, 3316, 3322, 3324, 3455, 3673, 3674, 3677, 3678, 3679, 3729, 3875, 3915, 3926, 3938, 3939, 3940
17	8588, 8590, 8592, 8593, 8594, 8597, 8598, 8599, 8600, 8601, 8602, 8603, 8604
24	5102, 5103, 5104, 5105, 5106, 5107, 5108, 5109, 5110, 5111
25	7586, 7593, 7596
37	6741, 6742, 6745, 6746, 6748, 6756, 6757, 6758, 6759, 6760, 6761, 6762, 6763, 6764, 6765, 6766, 6767, 6768, 6770, 6771, 6772, 6787, 6792, 6793, 6795, 6796, 6797, 6799, 6818, 6833, 6873, 6900, 6912, 6913, 6917, 6928, 6951, 6952
40	237, 238, 239, 240, 270, 271, 273, 280, 281, 282, 283, 284, 285, 286, 345, 346, 347, 352, 353, 355
46	139, 148, 153, 160, 164, 166, 168, 169, 170, 171, 172, 173, 175, 177, 178, 180, 182, 190, 192
47	1101, 1102, 1103, 1104, 1105, 1106, 1989, 1990, 1991, 1992, 1993, 1995, 1996, 1997, 1998, 1999
55	9002, 9005, 9008, 9011, 9014, 9017

Total 172

Gateshead Locomotive Allocation
1 January 1980

03	03056/059/061/064/066/069/078/079/094, 03107/111/170
08	08053/054/058/081/085, 08116/127/147/148/170/176, 08217/254/274, 08325/370/373, 08512/544/562, 08671, 08708/747/775, 08872/888
31	31120/122/129/139/184/186/187, 31280/288/289, 31406/418
37	37003/005/013/029/030/032/058/059/061/062/063/065/066/068/071/073, 37076/078/082/083, 37100/101/106/195/199, 37212/216/242/250
40	40052/056/057/058/068/074/077
46	46029-056
47	47401-420

Total 134

Top:
In 1887 the NER sent 2-4-0 No 1324 to the Newcastle Exhibition. This was T. W. Worsdell's first passenger engine design since coming to the NER from the GER. It was a two-cylinder compound built at Gateshead, and although the next design (Class F) retained the Worsdell/von Borries compound system, Worsdell changed to the 4-4-0 wheel arrangement. No 1324 was specially painted for the Exhibition and carried T. W. Worsdell's version of the North Eastern's coat of arms.
K. Hoole Collection

Above:
T. W. Worsdell's first design of shunting engine was Class E, introduced in February 1887, but all 120 of these engines were built at Darlington. No 275 in T. W. Worsdell livery was photographed at Redheugh c1890. This was a favourite location for an early Tyneside railway photographer as there are numerous views of NER engines at this venue on the south bank of the Tyne west of Gateshead, with the works of the Newcastle & Gateshead Gas Co often visible in the background on the other side of the river. *K. Hoole Collection*

Top:
From Class E developed Class E1 with the same boiler but with wheels 6in smaller in diameter. In 1960 two engines were painted green with the NER and BR crests on the side tanks. No 68736 was photographed shunting at the west end of Newcastle Central. *Ian S. Carr*

Above:
The Class U 0-6-2T was introduced by Wilson Worsdell in 1902 and No 1667 was also photographed at Redheugh. *K. Hoole Collection*

Heaton Locomotive Allocation
6 December 1923

LNER Class	NER Class		
B13	S	4-6-0	752, 757, 759, 761, 1077, 2002, 2004, 2005
B15	S2	4-6-0	787, 788, 791, 795, 796, 797, 798, 825
B16	S3	4-6-0	840, 841, 842, 843, 846, 906, 914, 922, 930, 932, 934, 937, 943, 1372, 1373, 1379, 1383
C6	V	4-4-2	532, 649, 742, 784, 1680, 1776
C7	Z	4-4-2	710, 2195, 2196, 2197, 2200, 2203, 2211
D20	R	4-4-0	1078, 1207, 1232
G5	O	0-4-4T	384, 1316, 1687, 1745, 1748, 1754, 1755, 1762, 1791, 1793, 1838, 1865, 1866, 1886, 1918, 2086, 2096
G6	BTP	0-4-4T	62, 323, 416
H1	D	4-4-4T	1499, 1501, 1519, 1523, 1529, 2157, 2158, 2159, 2160
J21	C	0-6-0	31, 182, 360, 424, 480, 513, 538, 539, 558, 569, 667, 871, 877, 960, 962, 974, 992, 994, 1071, 1187, 1309, 1336, 1508, 1510, 1565, 1576, 1608, 1801, 1813, 1816, 1818
J26	P2	0-6-0	342
J27	P3	0-6-0	2338
44	44	0-6-0T	94
J71	E	0-6-0T	103, 248, 275, 280, 400, 403, 572, 969, 1123, 1144
J72	E1	0-6-0T	1732, 1733, 1734, 1747, 1749, 2320
J73	L	0-6-0T	550
J76	124	0-6-0T	599
N8	B	0-6-2T	271, 504, 862
X3	190	2-2-4T	190
Y7	H	0-4-0T	519, 982
Electric ES1	Bo-Bo		1, 2
Electric EE1	4-6-4		13

Total 139

Heaton Locomotive Allocation
1 January 1939

LNER Class		
A1	4-6-2	2579 *Dick Turpin*, 2581 *Neil Gow*, 2582 *Sir Hugo*
A3	4-6-2	2544 *Lemberg*, 2578 *Bayardo*, 2580 *Shotover*
A4	4-6-2	4464 *Bittern*
B15	4-6-0	795, 796, 798, 825
C7	4-4-2	710, 2197, 2200, 2210, 2211
G5	0-4-4T	405, 1687, 1745, 1748, 1755, 1783, 1791, 1918
J21	0-6-0	209, 294, 513, 569, 778, 871, 965, 1565, 1576, 1608, 1812, 1816
J27	0-6-0	1035, 1039, 1189, 1204, 1227, 2340
J39	0-6-0	1482, 1483, 1504, 1505
J71	0-6-0T	177, 275, 280, 403, 572, 1123, 1834
J72	0-6-0T	1732, 1733, 1734, 1747, 1749, 2337
K3	2-6-0	36, 1106, 1117, 1118, 1119, 1322, 1325, 1332, 1333, 1339, 1389, 1391, 1392, 1394
N10	0-6-2T	89, 429, 1710, 1711
Q5	0-8-0	669, 767
V1	2-6-2T	402, 417, 418, 422, 428, 440, 461, 477, 486, 487, 497, 498
V2	2-6-2	4778, 4779, 4781, 4783, 4804
ES1	Bo-Bo	1, 2

Total 98

Heaton Locomotive Allocation
1 October 1954

Class		
A1	4-6-2	60116 *Hal o' the Wynd*, 60126 *Sir Vincent Raven*, 60127 *Wilson Worsdell*
A2	4-6-2	60511 *Airborne*, 60517 *Ocean Swell*, 60539 *Bronzino*
A3	4-6-2	60069 *Sceptre*, 60072 *Sunstar*, 60073 *St Gatien*, 60077 *The White Knight*, 60080 *Dick Turpin*, 60083 *Sir Hugo*, 60085 *Manna*, 60088 *Book Law*, 60091 *Captain Cuttle*, 60092 *Fairway*
D20	4-4-0	62387
J21	0-6-0	65035, 65039, 65110
J27	0-6-0	65869, 65873, 65882, 65893
J39	0-6-0	64703, 64853, 64856, 64915, 64916, 64923, 64945

J71	0-6-0T	68245, 68251, 68262, 68263, 68264, 68278	
J72	0-6-0T	68682, 68702, 68708, 68725, 68738, 68742, 68747, 69027, 69028	
J77	0-6-0T	68428	
J94	0-6-0ST	68014, 68021	
K3	2-6-0	61818, 61875, 61904, 61906, 61927, 61932, 61984, 61986, 61987	
N8	0-6-2T	69377	
V1	2-6-2	67635, 67637, 67640, 67641, 67642, 67645, 67646, 67647, 67651, 67654, 67673	
V2	2-6-2	60801, 60806, 60810, 60811, 60812, 60833, 60835 *The Green Howard Alexandra, Princess of Wales's Own Yorkshire Regiment*, 60885, 60886, 60887, 60891, 60910, 60939, 60942, 60944, 60945, 60952	
V3	2-6-2T	67652	
4MT	2-6-0	43016, 43030, 43043, 43070, 43129	
ES1	Bo-Bo	26500, 26501	

Total 95

Borough Gardens Locomotive Allocation
6 December 1923

LNER Class	NER Class		
398	398	0-6-0	79, 196, 389, 391, 396, 398, 417, 805, 1297, 1429, 1450
J22	59	0-6-0	522, 1481
J24	P	0-6-0	1828, 1841, 1898, 1900, 1937, 1938
J25	P1	0-6-0	1986, 2000, 2133, 2141
J26	P2	0-6-0	835, 881
J27	P3	0-6-0	1004, 2340, 2344
J71	E	0-6-0T	54, 70, 179, 254, 301, 482, 501, 1690, 1796, 1833, 1834, 1862
J72	E1	0-6-0T	2187, 2188, 2189, 2190, 2191
Q5	T1	0-8-0	654
Q6	T2	0-8-0	1251, 1335, 2227, 2236, 2247, 2279, 2287, 2288, 2290, 2291, 2292, 2294, 2295, 2300, 2302

Total 61

Borough Gardens Locomotive Allocation
1 January 1939

J24	0-6-0	1829, 1846, 1899, 1937, 1945, 1946, 1954, 1960
J25	0-6-0	2133
J27	0-6-0	1003, 1004, 1007, 1393, 1686
J72	0-6-0T	1770, 2187, 2188, 2189, 2191, 2329, 2330
N8	0-6-2T	293, 503, 1105, 1127
Q6	0-8-0	1251, 1253, 1254, 1278, 1292, 1311, 1335, 2213, 2214, 2227, 2236, 2261, 2268, 2279, 2287, 2290, 2291, 2292, 2294, 2295, 2300, 2301, 2302

Total 48

Borough Gardens Locomotive Allocation
1 October 1954

B1	4-6-0	61319, 61320, 61321
J25	0-6-0	65645, 65657, 65661, 65686, 65705, 65728
J39	0-6-0	64700, 64707, 64710, 64713, 64846, 64851, 64854, 64921, 64926, 64927, 64931, 64936
J71	0-6-0T	68287, 68289, 68316
J72	0-6-0T	68694, 68697, 68705, 68728, 68730, 68736, 68737, 69017
Q6	0-8-0	63342, 63350, 63354, 63358, 63366, 63377, 63384, 63386, 63400, 63402, 63408, 63431, 63434, 63444, 63456, 63458

Total 48

Blaydon Locomotive Allocation
6 December 1923

LNER Class	NER Class		
B13	S	4-6-0	756, 766, 755
D20	R	4-4-0	2012
G5	O	0-4-4T	1169, 1691, 1702, 1751, 1783, 1840, 1868
H1	D	4-4-4T	1328, 1329, 1330, 1521, 1522
J21	C	0-6-0	315, 458, 965, 1122, 1188, 1301, 1337, 1338, 1557, 1564, 1588, 1607, 1609, 1610, 1611, 1613, 1812
J24	P	0-6-0	1854, 1934, 1955
J25	P1	0-6-0	1985, 2137
J26	P2	0-6-0	434, 1369

Top:
For passenger work T. W. Worsdell introduced a 2-4-2T in 1886 — his first design for the NER — and two engines survived until 1938 on Newcastle to South Shields and Sunderland services. When the South Shields line was electrified they were both withdrawn from Tyne Dock Shed, where No 420 was photographed by W. Leslie Good; the other engine was No 40. *W. L. Good*

Above:
The two most successful NER tank engine designs for passenger work both had the 0-4-4T wheel arrangement — the 124 BTP engines by Edward Fletcher and the 110 Class O engines by Wilson Worsdell. This is Class O No 2093 at Newcastle in NER days. *T. G. Hepburn*

Above:
The North Eastern had one class of 4-4-4T, which first appeared in 1913. They were used extensively in the Newcastle area, with five at Gateshead, five at Blaydon, and nine at Heaton in 1923. This view of No 1526, with the 104,000gal water tank in the background, was taken at the west end of Central station in 1926 and shows the engine and vans with primitive protection against stone-throwing strikers and sympathisers. *BR*

Below:
In their rebuilt form as Class A8 these handsome engines were used on Tyneside and No 69893 was photographed at Gateshead shed in 1955.
S. E. Teasdale

J27	P3	0-6-0	1039, 2341, 2348
J71	E	0-6-0T	161, 177, 181, 242, 244, 252, 268, 272, 1861
J72	E1	0-6-0T	2325, 2335, 2336, 2337
J77	290	0-6-0T	958
N8	B	0-6-2T	348, 1072
N9	N	0-6-2T	1645
N10	U	0-6-2T	1109
Q6	T2	0-8-0	2222, 2238, 2258, 2260, 2261, 2262, 2266, 2267, 2269
Y7	H	0-4-0T	983

Total 71

K1	2-6-0	62002, 62006, 62010, 62021, 62022, 62023, 62024, 62025, 62026, 62027, 62028, 62029, 62030
Q6	0-8-0	63353, 63356, 63363, 63376, 63381, 63385, 63390, 63391, 63394, 63398, 63399, 63403, 63412, 63413, 63428, 63432, 63441
V1	2-6-2T	67639, 67657, 67658
V3	2-6-2T	67636, 67653, 67656
4MT	2-6-0	43126

Total 69

Blaydon Locomotive Allocation
1 January 1939

LNER Class

D20	4-4-0	2027, 2028
G5	0-4-4T	1762, 1868, 2096
J21	0-6-0	123, 1122, 1337, 1557, 1564, 1588, 1607, 1609, 1610, 1611
J39	0-6-0	1418, 1425, 1429, 1451, 1452, 1454, 1466, 1488, 1563, 1584
J71	0-6-0T	161, 244, 254, 268, 1861
J72	0-6-0T	2325, 2336
J77	0-6-0T	324, 1116
K3	2-6-0	33, 38, 46
Q6	0-8-0	2218, 2222, 2231, 2238, 2240, 2242, 2247, 2252, 2258, 2260, 2266, 2269, 2271, 2281
V1	2-6-2T	414, 419, 423, 446, 465, 479, 481, 484

Total 59

Blaydon Locomotive Allocation
1 October 1954

D20	4-4-0	62349
D49	4-4-0	62747 *The Percy*, 62771 *The Rufford*
G5	0-4-4T	67241, 67248, 67277, 67304, 67320, 67323, 67325, 67339
J21	0-6-0	65090
J39	0-6-0	64705, 64812, 64814, 64816, 64842, 64849, 64858, 64870
J21	0-6-0T	68267, 68273
J72	0-6-0T	68731, 69023, 69024, 69025, 69026
J94	0-6-0ST	68010, 68035, 68036, 68038, 68059

Bowes Bridge Locomotive Allocation
6 December 1923

LNER Class   *NER Class*

N8	B	0-6-2T	349
N10	U	0-6-2T	1138, 1683

Total 3

Bowes Bridge Locomotive Allocation
1 January 1939

LNER Class

N10	0-6-2T	1109, 1138

Total 2

Bowes Bridge Locomotive Allocation
1 October 1954

LNER Class

N10	0-6-2T	69097, 69100

Total 2

Top :
Less familiar on Tyneside was the goods 'A7' 4-6-2T but this one, No 1179, was fitted in 1935 with vacuum brake equipment for use on passenger trains on the steeply graded lines to Consett.
W. L. Good

Above:
Favourites for the Tyne Commission Quay boat trains were the 'A5' 4-6-2T engines — the Great Central design to which 13 engines for the North Eastern Area were built on Tyneside in 1925/26. This is No 1750 on the down 'Norseman' at Platform 10 at Central station on 5 September 1936. *W. B. Greenfield*

Above:
The NER produced the first Class S 4-6-0 in 1899, and a slightly modified design, known sometimes as Class S/07, in 1908. This is one of the 1908 engines, No 759, on a down goods at Killingworth.
Photomatic

Below:
Class S3, the North Eastern's final design of 4-6-0, became well known as Class B16 because these engines worked all over the North-East on passenger, freight and mineral trains. In 1923 there were 27 engines divided between Gateshead (10) and Heaton (17) but in BR days they tended to be allocated to sheds further south. However, in the mid-1950s a number were working from Heaton, such as No 61440 seen crossing the King Edward Bridge on an up goods on 8 October 1955. *K. Hoole*

Summary of Locomotive Allocations
at Peripheral sheds

Shed	Class	1923	1939	1954
Hexham	G5	4	4	6
	Y1	–	1	–
	J21	–	–	1
	J36	–	1	–
Alnmouth	1440	1	–	–
	D17/1	1	1	–
	D20	–	4	5
	D22	1	–	–
	E5	2	–	–
	F8	3	–	–
	J21	2	1	–
	J22	1	–	–
	J39	–	–	4
	N10	1	1	–
Percy Main	398	3	–	–
	J24	3	–	–
	J25	3	3	–
	J26	1	–	–
	J27	20	14	22
	J77	1	–	–
	J78	1	–	–
Tyne Dock	F8	7	–	–
	G5	–	5	–
	J21	2	–	–
	J22	1	–	–
	J24	5	–	–
	J25	8	9	6
	J26	2	7	–
	J27	5	–	–
	J39	–	2	–
	J71	8	5	2
	J72	4	2	5
	J73	2	–	–
	J77	2	–	–
	N8	–	–	1
	N9	–	2	3
	N10	–	–	1
	O1	–	–	5
	Q5	1	2	–
	Q6	32	9	6
	Q7	1	4	15
	T1	5	2	2
	WD	–	–	4
	Y3	–	2	–
	Y7	9	5	–
Durham	398	1	–	–
	1440	3	–	–
	G5	–	4	4
	J21	2	–	–
	J22	1	–	–

Above left:

Like the 'B16s', the 'B1s' were everywhere! On this occasion No 1015 *Duiker* of York was photographed in Platform 9 at Central station on 1 January 1948. The crew of No 1015, and other conveniently handy locomen, were posed on the front of No 1015 to celebrate the nationalisation of the railways! The driver of No 1015, Wilf Simpson of York (third from left), was a dedicated locomotive man who received his early footplate experience at Bridlington shed on ex-North Eastern 4-4-0s of various types. *K. Hoole Collection*

Left:

No work on Newcastle would be complete without mention of the North Eastern Atlantics, which put in such a lot of work northwards to Edinburgh and southwards to York. However, No 2212 differed from the other 49 Class Z engines in having 'Uniflow' cylinders. Here is No 2212 backing on to a Pullman train in platform 10, to work it to Leeds Central via Harrogate. *W. L. Good*

Above:

Less successful were the Raven Pacifics; this is the pioneer engine No 2400 *City of Newcastle*, at Gateshead shed. *K. Hoole Collection/Real Photos*

Below:

Main line diesel locomotives have been illustrated in the various chapters but space must be found to acknowledge the work of the various diesel shunters — particularly the very successful 350hp Class 08. Here Class 03 No 03112 and Class 08 No 08886 await their next call of duty at the west end of Central station on 23 June 1984. *Ian S. Carr*

12 Railcars

An unidentified Clayton steam railcar was tried on the Ponteland branch in 1926, but it was not until 1928 that six new cars were delivered from the Lincoln makers, namely No 285 *Rapid*, No 287 *Royal Sovereign*, No 289 *Wellington*, No 296 *Wonder*, No 2101 *Union*, and No 2110 *Comet*. All the cars were stationed at Heaton shed where they were joined by No 41 from the Southern Area, which later

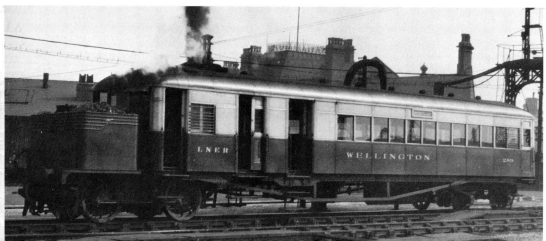

Above:
The three Armstrong Whitworth cars — *Tyneside Venturer, Northumbrian* and *Lady Hamilton* — made numerous demonstration runs in the Newcastle area before being purchased by the LNER — *Tyneside Venturer* for £7,500 and the other two for £5,500 each. *K. Hoole Collection*

received the name *Pilot*, and changed its number to No 2121. The Clayton cars, which were not a great success, also worked north to Morpeth, and on the Derwent Valley branch to Blackhill; one turn also took a car to Leamside. However, difficulties in obtaining spares and the general unsuitability of the cars led to them being restricted to one service and, as they were unsuited to replace Sentinel cars, only a very small mileage was being obtained: this led to suggestions that they should be scrapped.

In fact No 285 *Rapid* was withdrawn in September 1932 (although not broken up until some years later), and No 2110 *Comet* was transferred to the Southern Area in 1935 and subsequently withdrawn from Norwich in 1937. The remaining five cars were all withdrawn from Heaton shed in 1936. No 41 was originally in the standard teak coach livery but it was repainted in the early railcar livery of red and cream in February 1929; the other cars were apparently delivered in the red and cream livery.

Sentinel steam railcars were tried in the southern part of the North Eastern Area in 1925, but the first two cars purchased by the LNER worked in the Lowestoft area and it was not until 1927 that No 22 — later named *Brilliant* — appeared at Newcastle on Ponteland and North Wylam workings. It too was originally in the teak livery before adopting red and cream, and eventually green and cream. Heaton shed acquired other two-cylinder cars at various times, such as No 244 *True Briton* in 1928, and again in 1939, and

No 254 *Phoenix*, also in 1939. However the depot relied mainly on six-cylinder cars, such as No 2198 *Times*, No 2257 *Defiance*, No 2261 *Diligence*, No 2270 *Independent*, No 2271 *Industry*, and No 2276 *North Briton*. In the summer of 1937 Heaton shed turned out three Sentinel cars each weekday, all three working to North Wylam, Blackhill and Prudhoe. The last Sentinel car to be allocated to Heaton was No 2276 *North Briton* which was transferred to West Auckland on 13 November 1943, thus bringing to an end 25 years of work in the Newcastle area.

When in the early 1930s Messrs Armstrong-Whitworth of Scotswood decided to produce diesel locomotives and railcars, many of their products were tried out in the Newcastle area, running over LNER lines. These included diesel-electric shunting locomotives and a large 1-Co-1 diesel-electric which underwent extensive trials on freight trains on the main line in 1933/34 and also worked some demonstration runs on trains conveying invited passengers. Best known were the three 60-seat 250hp diesel-electric railcars and the 57-seat railbus; the cars were named *Tyneside Venturer, Lady Hamilton* and *Northumbrian*, but the railbus never received the distinction of being named. The first car was demonstrated in the Newcastle area at the end of 1931 and made some press runs before going into regular service in January 1932. All three cars were eventually purchased by the LNER — *Tyneside Venturer* for £7,500 and the other two for £5,500 each. The railbus cost £4,370 but was sold to the LNER for £2,500. The larger cars were fitted with drawgear and buffers and weighed 42ton 10cwt, but the lightweight railbus was not equipped for hauling a tail load and weighed only 19tons 12cwt. All four cars were withdrawn in 1939 and there was a gap of 16 years before the British Railways Derby-built cars appeared in November 1955.